Therapeutic Foster Care

Critical Issues

EDITED BY

ROBERT P. HAWKINS, PH.D.

AND

JAMES BREILING, PH.D.

Child Welfare League of America
Washington, D.C.

CHILD WELFARE LEAGUE OF AMERICA, INC.
440 First Street, NW, Suite 310, Washington, DC 20001-2085

CURRENT PRINTING (last digit)
10 9 8 7 6 5 4 3 2 1

Cover design by Sherry Howard
Text design by Rose Jacobowitz

Printed in the United States of America

ISBN 0-87868-355-0

Library of Congress Cataloging-in-Publication Data

Therapeutic foster care : critical issues / edited by Robert P.
  Hawkins and James Breiling.
      p.   cm.
    Presentations made at a small conference held in 1984 in
  Pittsburgh, Pa., sponsored jointly by the National Institute of
  Mental Health, Antisocial and Violent Behavior Branch and the
  Pressley Ridge School.
    Includes bibliographies.
    ISBN 0-87868-355-0 : $26.95
    1. Child psychotherapy—Residential treatment—Congresses.
  2. Mentally handicapped children—Rehabilitation—Congresses.
  3. Foster home care—Psychological aspects—Congresses.
  I. Hawkins, Robert P., 1931–   . II. Breiling, James.
  III. National Institute of Mental Health (U.S.). Antisocial and
  Violent Behavior Branch.
  RJ504.5.T49   1989
  618.92'89—dc19   88-30216
                                                                  CIP

Contents

Preface

THIS BOOK GREW out of a small conference sponsored jointly by the National Institute of Mental Health Antisocial and Violent Behavior Branch and the Pressley Ridge Schools in Pittsburgh, Pennsylvania. The conference was held in 1984 and attended by approximately 30 key staff from three well-established, empirically and behaviorally oriented therapeutic foster care programs in the eastern United States, plus researchers from around the country concerned with better service to children and youth. The conference convinced all of us present that this general model—involving alternative families in a professional kind of role, under the training and guidance of mental health and child care professionals—held great potential for humane, effective, and comprehensive intervention in the lives of disturbed and conduct-disordered youngsters and their families.

Although it was clear that no program had yet developed the strategies and procedures for fully achieving that potential, it was also clear that there were programs on the right track, where innovation, excellence, program evaluation, and continued program improvement were the norm. It was decided that the time was right for sharing the general strategy of treating youngsters and their families through a professional treatment parent model, showing what three established, successful, empirically-based programs were doing, and discussing issues surrounding such programs. Toward that end, three volumes were written, this being one.

One of the three volumes (by John Carenen, an ex-treatment parent and writer) is a moving novel about two boys who, along with their parents, are having serious problems. These boys are served by a therapeutic foster care program. Realistically, in the story, the intervention requires persistent, creative, committed effort, but does not achieve complete success. That is the reality of our current level of intervention technology; but there is enough success to convince us that this minimally restrictive, humane, and relatively comprehensive general model is well worth pursuing and refining.

A second volume (by Pamela Meadowcroft and Barbara Trout) provides a fairly detailed description of how three excellent programs—People Places in Virginia, Professional Parenting in North Carolina, and PRYDE in Pennsylvania, West Virginia, and Maryland—are conducted. The various chapters are written by persons actually conducting these programs and describe the components of the programs, such as recruiting potential treatment parents, training and supervising treatment parents, the treatment given youngsters, services to the youngsters' parents, and program evaluation.

The present volume selects several important issues relevant to achieving the full potential of therapeutic foster care and provides advice from experts not directly involved in conducting such a program. Whereas the Meadowcroft and Trout text provides the nuts and bolts of conducting excellent programs, this volume provides more general guidelines. It includes the results of a nationwide study of therapeutic foster care programs, suggestions as to how to view such programs in comparison to other programs and public policies, advice on the conduct of training and supervision and on involvement of biological parents, research and advice on disseminating programs, and more.

Together, these three volumes should both motivate and guide professionals in the development of state-of-the-art therapeutic foster care programs for not only disturbed and conduct-disordered youngsters but also for youngsters and oldsters with other problems. This is our aim.

We wish to thank the Board of Trustees, the Executive Director, Wm. Clark Luster, and members of the staff of the Pressley Ridge Schools for their extensive and persistent support of both the 1984 conference and the development of these books. Thanks are similarly due to the boards of directors and staff members of People Places and Professional Parenting, and to Appalachian State University, where the latter agency is located as part of a larger agency, Bringing It All Back Home. This agency obtained the resources and provided the editorial guidance to get the novel written. A special thanks is due to the committed, persistent, creative, and hard-working treatment parents and staff members who make therapeutic foster care effective in helping thousands of youngsters all over the United States and Canada today. Finally, thanks to Mary Pendergrass, who cheerfully typed many revisions of parts of this volume, plus correspondence about all three.

Robert P. Hawkins, Ph.D.
James Breiling, Ph.D.

Contributors

Craig H. Blakely, Ph.D., is Assistant Professor, Department of Psychology, Michigan State University, East Lansing, MI.

Brad Bryant, M.P.A., is Director of Research and Training, People Places, Inc., Staunton, VA.

Thomas N. Carros, M.S.W., is Director, Allegheny County Children and Youth Services, Pittsburgh, PA.

Daniel L. Daly, Ph.D., is Director, National Family Home Program, Father Flanagan's Boys' Home, Boys Town, NE.

William S. Davidson, II, Ph.D., is Professor of Psychology and Chair, Ecological Psychology Graduate Training Program, Michigan State University, East Lansing, MI.

James G. Emshoff, Ph.D., is Associate Professor, Department of Psychology, Georgia State University, Atlanta, GA.

Robert M. Friedman, Ph.D., is Professor, Florida Mental Health Institute, University of Florida, Tampa, FL.

Rand Gottschalk, M.A., is Senior Consultant, Personnel Designs, Inc., Grosse Point, MI.

Robert P. Hawkins, Ph.D., is Professor and Coordinator of Child Clinical Training, Psychology Department, West Virginia University, Morgantown, WV.

Daniel Krikston, M.S.W., is Project Director, Specialized Foster Home Care Program, Allegheny County Children and Youth Services, Pittsburgh, PA.

Anthony N. Maluccio, D.S.W., is Professor, School of Social Work, University of Connecticut, West Hartford, CT.

Jeffrey P. Mayer, Ph.D., is Analyst, Program Evaluation and Methodology Division, U.S. General Accounting Office, Washington, DC.

David Roitman, Ph.D., is Researcher, Industrial Technology Institute, Ann Arbor, MI.

Neal Schmitt, Ph.D., is Professor, Department of Psychology and Management, Michigan State University, East Lansing, MI.

Robert D. Snodgrass, Ph.D., is Executive Director, People Places, Inc. Staunton, VA.

James K. Whittaker, Ph.D., is Professor of Social Work, University of Washington, Seattle, WA.

I

The Origins, Nature, and Promise of Therapeutic Foster Care

Introduction to
Part 1

I IN THIS SECTION of the book Robert Hawkins suggests the characteristics that define therapeutic foster care (TFC), pointing out that TFC includes programs that vary widely on several important dimensions. After briefly describing the historical developments that appear to have led to TFC's emergence and current popularity, Hawkins shows how TFC compares to a less restrictive alternative with which it is likely to be confused by both professionals and lay persons—foster family care—and how it compares to a more restrictive alternative—group residential treatment centers.

He then identifies seven dimensions along which TFC programs appear to vary widely and which he considers crucial in determining the intensity of treatment actually provided by a program, defining intensity as a combination of potency and breadth. Finally, he offers a three-dimensional matrix in which all treatment (or other intervention) programs can be compared, using two positive dimensions and one negative: potency, breadth, and restrictiveness.

Robert Snodgrass and Brad Bryant describe a study of 49 TFC programs in the United States and Canada. Most TFC programs appear to develop with little awareness of what other TFC programs are like; as a result, these programs may be little more than intensive foster family care, failing to achieve the treatment intensity that Hawkins identifies. Snodgrass and Bryant's research provides the first database regarding what other TFC programs do, how they do it, and for whom.

Their study provides data on such variables as the date of origin for each program, its mission, size, funding, costs, types of clients, length of stay, program parents and their recruitment and selection, preservice and inservice training, pay to program parents, staff responsibilities, services to biological parents, and follow-up services. It even provides suggestive evidence regarding programs' ability to divert youngsters from more restrictive placements.

Finally, Snodgrass and Bryant have generously provided the addresses of the 48 agencies that responded to their survey. This should be useful to other researchers.

The Snodgrass and Bryant data indicate that, on some dimensions, many programs are at the treatment-intensive end of the continuum described by Hawkins. On other dimensions, there are apparently few programs at the intensive end of the continuum. We simply have no information yet about where programs are on some dimensions; perhaps further research will reveal this.

It seems likely that the 48 programs that responded to the survey are generally the best of the 129 programs to which questionnaires were sent, so the data cannot be construed to represent all TFC programs. But the information that these researchers have provided is an invaluable resource for others who are beginning or conducting TFC programs, and one of the few studies extant of TFC.[1]

[1] Recent interest in, and growth of TFC programs led to a successful United States conference on TFC in 1985, in Asheville, NC, sponsored by the National Institute of Mental Health and Appalachian State University, and attended by more than 100 professionals from every part of the nation. International conferences on TFC were held in Minneapolis and Calgary in 1987 and 1988, respectively, with over 300 persons attending each. At the 1988 conference, Nutter, Hudson, and Galaway presented a further survey study in which they used the Snodgrass and Bryant mailing list, plus other promising addresses. They obtained responses from 157 TFC programs. As a result of these conferences a new organization is forming of persons interested in TFC. Persons or agencies wishing to join the organization should contact Ms. Joan Riebel, Director, Family Alternatives, 416 E. Hennepin Ave. #218, Minneapolis, MN 55414.

The Nature and Potential of Therapeutic Foster Family Care Programs

ROBERT P. HAWKINS

I N THE PAST TEN or 12 years therapeutic foster family care (TFC) programs have grown rapidly. They have served a wide variety of children and adolescents, including the retarded, the moderately disturbed or disturbing, the severely disturbed or disturbing, the delinquent, and even the medically fragile. Although this paper includes all but the last of these, its emphasis is on the disturbed and disturbing groups, which are the clientele served by the majority of TFC programs. Estimating from the data of Snodgrass and Bryant, elsewhere in this volume, there are approximately 250 to 500 or more TFC programs in the United States, with more appearing each month. TFC is clearly a treatment modality whose time has come.

This paper defines what TFC is, suggests how it has become so popular, and identifies what its potential may be. TFC is defined generally at first, but is later considerably elaborated in order to suggest important dimensions calling for the attention of those who would develop or evaluate a TFC program.

A General Definition of Therapeutic Foster Care

TFC has gone by many names: specialized foster family care, special foster care, treatment foster care, individualized residential treatment, and others. As argued later, the name does matter, but TFC programs all seem to have certain general characteristics in common: (a) they involve a youngster being placed out-of-home with an alternative family; (b) the alternative family, here called the TFC family, is more carefully selected than are regular foster families; (c) the TFC family is given some kind of preservice education or training and often inservice education or training as well; (d) the TFC family is supervised and/or assisted more intensively than regular foster families, with about six to 20 families per professional [Snodgrass and Bryant, this volume]; and (e) the TFC family is reimbursed at a rate between the reimbursement rate of regular foster parents and the salaries of the professional staff members who supervise them.

The goals and specific character of TFC programs very widely. As Hawkins et al. [1985] point out:

> some authors (e.g., Barnes 1980) view specialized foster care
> [TFC, here] as a "variation on a theme" (p. 6) of foster care
> and, thus, not as providing treatment but only providing an
> unusually good, tolerant home for a disturbed, disturbing, or
> handicapped youngster. Others view it as a more planned
> daily experience and systematic intervention that constitutes
> or approximates treatment (e.g., Bauer and Heinke 1976;
> Freeman 1978; Levin, Rubenstein, and Streiner 1976).

These differences among programs are analyzed later in this paper.

The Rise of TFC Programs

There appear to be at least ten identifiable streams of development that have contributed to the current popularity of TFC. In some TFC programs the effects of all of these streams are evident; in others the effects of only a few are seen. Each stream is described briefly; the description of the first four streams is adapted largely from Bryant [1980].

Foster Family Care

Foster family care was begun in this country in the mid-1800s with the shipping of groups of city children to the midwest on trains, for "placing out" to farms and small town homes. By 1935 foster family care was so widely accepted that federal money was assigned to that purpose under the Social Security Act. Although foster family care has come under criticism on several grounds [e.g., Fanshel and Shinn 1978; Pardeck 1982], it is still widely accepted and being improved.

The influence of this stream on TFC is obvious, since most TFC programs are conducted under foster family care regulations, though not all. Further, most TFC programs are probably conducted by personnel who previously (or concurrently) have conducted regular foster family care; they may bring the assumptions and expectations learned in conducting foster family care. As a result, many TFC programs appear to be only slightly intensified versions of regular foster family care.

Institutional Care for Children

The almshouses, which housed persons of all ages and with diverse problems in the mid-1800s, were gradually replaced by orphan asylums and state institutions serving only children. By the turn of the century, special institutions were being established for special groups of children: retarded, delinquent, physically handicapped, and so forth. These were probably precursors to the development of residential treatment centers, which seem to have more directly contributed to TFC.

Residential Treatment Centers

By the 1940s a somewhat more homelike and therapeutically oriented institution for children and youths was becoming common: the residential treatment center. These centers usually have cottages or similar living units staffed by child care workers who have little previous formal training for their roles and who participate, with other staff members, in some form of milieu treatment, often under the supervision of mental health professionals. Often the latter also provide some kind of direct, office-based, weekly sessions of treatment, such as individual counseling, group therapy, or family therapy. These centers' milieu programming have contributed directly to TFC. As will be reiterated later, some of the procedures used to change client behavior in residential treatment centers and outpatient parent training are now in frequent use in TFC.

Outpatient Treatment of Children and Their Families

Beginning early in this century, child guidance clinics were established as a service for delinquent children and adolescents. These were more highly professionalized than earlier services, with a psychiatrist, a psychologist, and a social worker typically involved in each case. The psychiatrist usually met with the youngster, conducting insight-oriented psychotherapy or occasionally other modes such as play therapy or group therapy. Initially, the psychologist's role was primarily testing, but gradually it too came to include psychotherapy with the youngster. The social worker typically worked with the parents—essentially conducting a form of psychotherapy but not usually permitted to call it such—and often made telephone or even direct contact with the youngster's school or other community agencies as it became evident to mental health professionals that the problem was not just the child's.

The child guidance clinic developed methods for individualized assessment and treatment, usually based on psychoanalytic concepts; gradually, it came to serve a wide variety of adjustment difficulties. The contributions of this stream to TFC include recognition of the youngster as deserving of intensive individual treatment comparable to adults and the clear acknowledgment that the youngster was not the only one with a problem; his or her ecology held some responsibility. However, clinical services were still restricted almost totally to the office, where one-to-one verbal interactions were the predominant mode of treatment.

Service to the Child's Ecology

The 1960s saw increasing recognition that child treatment focused too exclusively on the child, neglecting to adequately influence the home, school, and neighborhood ecology. This concern was particularly evident in the programs established by Nicholas Hobbs and colleagues [Hobbs 1966, 1982] called Project Re-Education, or simply Re-Ed. In Re-Ed, energetic, educated young people with no particular mental health training not only taught and cared for children and adolescents but also went out into the chidren's homes, schools, and neighborhoods to intervene there until an adequate accommodation was achieved between the youngster's ecology and behavior. Further, youngsters were kept involved with their families by regular weekend home visits. The influence of such ecological thinking on TFC is the recognition that much can be accomplished of a therapeutic nature with little direct involvement of a mental health professional, and that every aspect of the youngster's ecology is a legitimate area for intervention. However, the youngster was still being served in a group environment that was fairly segregated from community living.

Parent Training

An extension of the ecological and paraprofessional emphases was the discovery and experimental demonstration in the 1950s and 1960s that the parents of a youngster with adjustment problems could be trained to play a therapeutic role with that youngster [e.g., Hawkins et al. 1966; O'Dell 1974; Patterson et al. 1967; Wahler et al. 1965; Williams 1959]. Although the success of putting parents in a therapeutic role depends upon the many contingencies under which the parents live [Wahler 1980] and, no doubt, upon how much the youngster's problems are intertwined with the parents' problems, human service professionals have become optimistic about the potential that parents have for affecting their children's behavior in habilitative ways. Thus, programs like Project 12-Ways [Lutzker 1984], the Portage Project [Cochran and Shearer 1984], and Homebuilders [Kinney et al. 1977] have developed in which even parents of low educational and socioeconomic level are taught, among other things, to behave in more effective ways toward their children.

Growing Behavior-Change Technology

Over the past 25 years or so, an ever-increasing array of strategies, tactics, and procedures for affecting child behavior has been accumulating [e.g., Dangel and Polster 1984, 1988; Graziano and Mooney 1984; Kelly 1983]. The science of applied behavior analysis has stimulated much of this development [see any issue of *Journal of Applied Behavior Analysis*, or Catania and Brigham 1978], as illustrated in the research conducted at Achievement Place and in other settings involved in the development of the Teaching Family Model of group home care and treatment [Braukmann et al. 1980; Fixsen et al. 1973; Watson et al. 1980]. Applied behavior analysis has the advantages of being integrated with the basic science of behavior analysis in which the environment— as opposed to hypothesized inner mental or emotional variables—is consistently viewed as containing the primary, ultimate causes of behavior; so the clinician searches for environmental solutions, ones that he or she can directly manipulate. In addition, single-case strategies of research are typically employed by applied behavior analysts; these are highly compatible with clinical services as well as with the simple fact that every client is truly unique [Barlow et al. 1984; Hawkins, 1989].

Although some TFC programs emphasize behavior analytic strategies and procedures and many others use at least a few of the procedures [see Snodgrass and Bryant, this volume], behavior analysis is by no means the only source of clinical concepts and methods in TFC. For example, Gordon's [1970] communication approach and the Adlerian approach described by Dreikurs [1957] and Dinkmeyer and McKay [1973] are probably frequent sources of concepts and procedures.

Awareness of the Need for Child Mental Health Services

Thirty or forty years ago any discussion of mental health or mental illness was likely to deal only with issues and problems involving adults. Although childhood experiences were given great importance in describing the development of adult behavioral difficulties, thanks significantly to Freud's influence, the behavioral difficulties experienced during childhood were given little attention. Even today, most books on psychopathology devote the great majority of their pages to adult disorders; the latest version of the Diagnostic and Statistical Manual [American Psychiatric Association 1987] is primarily about adult disorders. More importantly, the clinical services for disturbed or disturbing children and adolescents are still so inadequate that Knitzer [1982] subtitled her book about this problem "The failure of public responsibility to children and adolescents in need of mental health services."

But progress is being made. Many journals and texts are now devoted exclusively or primarily to children and families with problems, including texts devoted to child psychopathology, assessment, or treatment; and the number grows steadily. Graduate training programs in clinical child psychology are becoming numerous, the National Institute of Mental Health (NIMH) has given priority recently to grants for training child clinicians, and services for children and adolescents are now being stimulated by a project entitled Child And Adolescent Services Program (CAASP), started in 1984 by NIMH "to support states in the development of interagency efforts to improve the systems under which the most troubled children and youth receive service" [Stroul and Friedman 1986], especially by interagency collaboration and the coordination of service-delivery systems.

Deinstitutionalization, Minimizing Restrictiveness, and Advocacy

For many decades there has been concern about the humaneness of treatment for disturbed persons, especially the custodial warehousing and inhumane treatment that often occurred in mental hospitals [Ullmann and Krasner 1975]. This finally led to a deinstitutionalization movement that rapidly gained momentum in the 1970s and is still in progress. Part of the movement is reflected in the emphasis on minimizing the restrictiveness of treatment programming through court rulings (beginning in 1966 with *Lake v. Cameron*), public policy, financial incentives, agency policy, and the practices of individual professionals. Another part of this movement, and one that sometimes goes beyond concern for only the humaneness of treatment to a concern about the effectiveness of treatment, is the development of client advocacy. This advocacy takes many forms and is conducted by different people, including the clients themselves, relatives, professional advocates, and citizen and professional organizations.

The result of all these efforts has been to create pressure for community-based services, especially low-restrictiveness services. TFC is such a service, and its recently explosive popularity is doubtless due significantly to such pressure.

Cost Cutting and Accountability

The final streams of development that seem to be promoting TFC and other community-based programs have to do with cost and, one hopes, cost effectiveness. For more than a decade the need for accountability in human services has been asserted, including social service, mental health, and education. Of course, accountability should imply the assessment of both cost and effect. Cost is usually interpreted to mean monetary cost. It is not too difficult to find an acceptable and simple way to calculate such a cost, but it is difficult to agree upon what effects are most important and how to measure them. Outcome measurement can be complicated and costly to implement, though it need not be [e.g., Fabry et al. 1987a; Fabry et al. 1987b; Hawkins et al. 1982; McSweeny et al. 1982]. The result is that accountability often means simply cost reduction.

Much of the actual pressure for cost reduction comes from those in the legislative or executive branches of government, whether at federal, state, or local levels. When the pressure takes the form of legislation, budget approval, per diem ceilings, and so forth, priorities are placed by bureaucrats on one kind of program versus another. Because TFC is inexpensive compared to the residential treatment centers, institutions, and group homes in which the youngsters would otherwise be placed, the development of TFC programs is being encouraged, and referrals from public agencies are usually ample to keep TFC programs viable, once established.

Thus, several historical developments and current concerns have made TFC possible, attractive, and probably at least as effective as most other placements. Of course, TFC is not the only type of program that has been made possible and attractive by these factors. Many community-based alternatives are being developed. One of the most noteworthy for children and youths is what Friedman elsewhere in this volume calls "intensive home-based services," in which professionals with skill at a wide range of interventions try to prevent out-of-home placement of youngsters at risk by intervening in the family and its community ecology. The Homebuilders' staff, in Tacoma, Washington, has found their intensive home-based intervention program effective in preventing placement and relatively low in cost [Kinney et al. 1977]. But, for many youngsters, out-of-home placement will be necessary, and TFC will be the placement of choice.

Achieving the Potential of TFC Through a Continuum of TFC Programs

I have read about, heard about, visited, and discussed many different TFC programs since Clark Luster and I—admittedly almost totally ignorant of what others had done or were doing in TFC already—designed and began such a program in 1980–1981 [Hawkins and Luster 1982]. I have come to believe that our substantial ignorance at that time was much more an advantage than a disadvantage, because we approached the problem without the usual baggage of assumptions regarding what was possible, what was necessary, what procedures would work, what one could expect of parents, what kind of staff members were important to hire, what kind of caseload would be appropriate, and so on. The result is that we invented a program that differed quite substantially from others, and, under the leadership of Pamela Meadowcroft, has grown rapidly, and has continued to develop. Perhaps many of the assumptions commonly made in developing TFC programs stand in the way of achieving their greatest potential.

To identify clearly TFC's promise it will first be compared with two alternative kinds of placements, one less restrictive and one more restrictive: foster family care and residential treatment centers.* Then a continuum of services within the general TFC concept will be described and various levels of TFC programming will be located on that continuum.

TFC Compared to Foster Family Care and Residential Treatment

Comparison to Foster Family Care. TFC is similar to foster family care in that (1) TFC is centered in the private home of a substitute family; (2) the substitute family has been evaluated and selected; (3) it is, in some degree, monitored and supported while fulfilling its child care role; and (4) the family is paid. There are at least four differences, however, between TFC and foster family care. The first three are differences of degree: (1) the evaluation criteria that a TFC family must meet are higher; (2) the amount of contact between the family and professional staff, and thus the amount of monitoring and support to the TFC parent, is much greater; and (3) the TFC family is paid much better, because they are necessariy providing a much more difficult service. The final difference is not always one of degree: (4) TFC families are always given some amount of education or training, while this is often not required of regular foster parents.

Comparison to Residential Treatment. Good TFC is also similar to the group residential treatment that is found in the better residential treatment centers and group homes, as Whittaker and Maluccio point out elsewhere in this volume. Both of them (1) use planned procedures to change behavior and (2) direct those procedures at individually selected goals. The direct treatment personnel (e.g., child care worker), while (3) not normally high credentialed mental health professionals, are (4) trained and supervised on the job, and (5) apply the planned procedures in approximately the same way to all clients. Further, (6) the procedures are applied throughout the day and night. These last four similarities between TFC and other residential treatment are also characteristics that differentiate them from outpatient, office-based therapies.

---

*I am indebted to Pamela Meadowcroft, and probably others, for parts of this analysis.

But TFC differs from group residential treatment in that (1) TFC is much more readily and fully individualized, since (2) only one or two client youngsters normally live in a treatment home. This nongrouping approach not only facilitates individualization but also avoids the modeling and reinforcement of maladaptive, often destructive or antisocial behavior that comes with grouping of disturbed and disturbing youngsters. TFC also avoids the relatively impersonal quality, and thus irresponsibility, that is typical in group living, especially group living in a building owned by an impersonal agency rather than a family. TFC also differs from group residential treatment in that (3) TFC is more personalized and consistent, because the treatment personnel do not change every eight hours; they are constant throughout the 24-hour day, month after month, developing a unique, involved relationship with the youngster, which has proven to be a very important contribution to effective treatment [e.g., Braukmann et al. 1984].

Dimensions Defining a Continuum of Therapeutic Foster Care

Although it is clear from the preceding that TFC programs share many similarities [see also Webb 1988], there are large and important differences among them. Some of the similarities and differences are evident in the research presented by Snodgrass and Bryant elsewhere in this volume.

There appear to be approximately seven dimensions of difference between one TFC program and another that have a substantial influence on the promise of these programs for effecting change in youngsters and their families, and that together may constitute a continuum of TFC in which programs at one end are capable of serving mildly disturbed/disturbing or retarded youngsters while programs at the other end can effectively serve more severely disturbed/disturbing or retarded youngsters. These dimensions compose a more general dimension that I will call "intensity of treatment" [cf. Hawkins and Luster 1982]. Each dimension will be described briefly, but no attempt will be made here to quantify them. No pretense is made that these seven, and only these seven, best define the continuum. The first purpose here is to point out that the variations among TFC programs are often consequential: some of them have substantial impact on the potency and comprehensiveness of treatment. The second purpose is to suggest some of the variations that have such an impact.

TFC Parent and Home Qualifications.　　In practice, foster family care has accepted a range of foster homes in which the foster parents at the lower end of the range are virtually illiterate, unambitious, uninformed about the community's resources (cultural, medical, occupational, social), uninformed about mental health, poorly organized, and rather ineffective at following through on planned routines [e.g., De-Fries et al. 1970]. Their homes are sometimes in neighborhoods where crime and violence are fairly frequent. Although such a home may still meet minimum standards for caring for a child or youth—because the foster parents may still be quite nurturant, moral, and protective of their children—it cannot qualify as a therapeutic home for TFC. Because of the importance of planned teaching (treatment) by TFC parents, it is essential that they learn the necessary procedures readily and follow through on plans communicated orally or in writing, which can be predicted to some degree by their level of verbal, educational, and occupational achievement. For that same reason, it is important that they be organized, informed about community resources, energetic, interested in a semiprofessional job, not too burdened by conflicting demands on their time and patience, resourceful at solving problems, and primarily rational and objective rather than emotional.

Because of the influence of peers and even neighbors, it is important that the TFC home be in a neighborhood where there are prosocial age mates, where crime is rare, where neighbors can be relied upon to report a youngster's misbehavior to his or her parents, and where homes are well kept. Because of the importance of the unplanned, incidental, often unconscious teaching the TFC parent (like any parent) does, it is helpful if the TFC parent has a few recreational and social interests and activities, good job skills, a good marital relationship, good relationships with other relatives and neighbors, a reasonably orderly home, skills at home maintenance, and wise consumer habits. For the same reason, it is important that any other youngsters in the TFC family be responsible, moral, reasonable, cooperative, fairly orderly, and so forth. Finally, because the client youngster's relationships with members of the TFC family, especially the TFC parents, are the foundation upon which much of the potency of all teaching depends [Braukmann et al. 1984; Wolf 1978], it is important that the parents enjoy youngsters, are responsive to them as individuals, have a pleasant sense of humor, have some interests that will engage youngsters, and are not authoritarian even though they are comfortable with asserting their legitimate authority when needed.

Obviously one cannot recruit and retain large numbers of TFC families that meet all of these criteria or perhaps even a majority of them. But the more effectively a TFC program does approximate such an ideal, the more potential it has to serve severely disturbed/disturbing or retarded youngsters effectively. Thus, TFC programs with documentation that their TFC homes approximate the ideal in several ways can be assumed to have at least the potential to provide an intensive (potent and broad) version of TFC.

TFC Parents Preservice and Inservice Training.   No matter how promising the TFC homes are, the fulfillment of that promise in terms of effective treatment depends upon where the program falls on other dimensions. The first of these is the TFC parent training. As Snodgrass and Bryant report elsewhere in this volume, TFC programs vary considerably in how they conduct both preservice and inservice training.

Beginning with preservice training, it is noteworthy that in some programs the emphasis is on learning *about* such topics as the relative roles of foster parents and foster care agencies or on child and adolescent development. This kind of verbal education, while relevant, seems of considerably lower priority than learning to *do* certain things under certain conditions, since it is the actions of TFC parents that directly affect youngsters, not the parents' verbal knowledge. Given that TFC parent training is, at best, extremely brief, especially when compared to the training of mental health professionals, and is not even required of each TFC parent in all programs, it seems that the highest priority should be placed on skill acquisition. This is why the model used by Daly and his colleagues for training group home parents is relevant to the training of TFC parents and is described in this volume.

Besides training TFC parents in skills rather than simply verbal information, a program that is intended to serve severely or even moderately disturbed or retarded youngsters needs to carry that training to prespecified performance criteria and document each TFC parent's achievement of each criterion. Otherwise there is no assurance that any particular TFC parent has mastered any particular skill. Unless the preservice training is programmed such that each person moves through it independently at his or her own pace—an expensive characteristic that has advantages but that no program appears to have attempted—attendance at training sessions must be mandatory and documented. From Snodgrass and Bryant's research reported elsewhere in this volume, it appears that training with all three of these characteristics—a skill emphasis, documented acquisition of critical skills, and mandatory attendance—is rare.

Perhaps the reason why some TFC programs have not emphasized the acquisition of specific skills in their preservice training is that they believe the TFC parents should carry out the treatment in their own unique way. This, however, seems to be a case of professionals avoiding the difficult decisions. It is always easy to excuse indecisiveness about what actions are highest priority by leaving them to the individuals who must act; but when those individuals have no professional training from which to generate and evaluate alternative courses of action, indecisiveness on the part of the professionals seems unjustifiable. There is ample research supporting the effectiveness of several treatment strategies and skills applicable in TFC homes; if a program is to achieve its potential, the professionals responsible for developing the preservice training should either be familiar with that research and technology or should employ others who are.

Regarding inservice or on-the-job training, Daly's paper in this volume is again relevant. No amount of preservice training will produce skilled TFC parent performance on the job. The stimulus conditions of the training setting are dramatically different from those that will exist in the home environment when a particular skill is called for, so the generalization of effects of the preservice training is unlikely [Martin and Pear 1988; Stokes and Baer 1977]. Even if the TFC parent does sometimes respond as desired, that response will not necessarily be immediately reinforced by the youngster or others; often it will be punished. The result will be that the appropriate parental behavior will rapidly disappear.

Thus, some kind of systematic in-home training seems necessary after a youngster has been placed in a TFC home, if a TFC program is to achieve its full potential. This should be combined with a systematic, periodic evaluation of the TFC parent's performance on the job. In the PRYDE program we have developed what may be the only systematic parent inservice evaluation (described briefly in Hawkins et al. 1985), but a systematic in-home training has yet to be developed.

Potency and Breadth of Direct Interventions with Youngsters. As suggested earlier, the content of the TFC parents' training has great impact on the program's ability to achieve change in a youngster's adjustment. If TFC parents use powerful teaching procedures aimed at individually selected and specific behaviors, more substantial and rapid changes can be achieved than if weak procedures are aimed at diffuse goals. Thus the skills to be taught and evaluated must be carefully selected if a program is to achieve high-intensity treatment, and there must be adequate professional resources for the collection of assessment information and its translation into an individual treatment plan.

Besides using potent procedures, a program serving seriously disturbed or retarded youngsters should be broad in its impact. It should routinely apply those potent procedures to any behavior in any aspect of the youngster's life, even his or her future life. Thus, to achieve maximum breadth of intervention the program must be ready to teach youngsters such varied skills and values as personal hygiene, posture, initiating and maintaining conversation, asking a teacher for assistance, refusing enticement toward misbehavior, ordering a restaurant meal, dieting, informing oneself about occupations, wise consumerism, returning excess change from a purchase, applying for a job, valuing one's reputation, and valuing other people's well-being. Of course, these will not be of equal priority for any youngster, and behaviors such as verbal abuse or noncompliance must be addressed early and effectively (though not necessarily through response-eliminative procedures; cf. Goldiamond 1974; Hawkins 1986). To be maximally effective, however, treatment must be as comprehensive as the youngster's present and probable future problems are. One of the great assets of TFC is that, with creative and energetic effort, intervention can be extremely broad, much broader than clinics, institutions, or even residential treatment centers can readily provide.

Potency and Breadth of Indirect Interventions, Those Addressing the Youngster's Ecology.   The task of assessment can be viewed as discovering where the client's behavior and the "template" [Hoier and Cone 1987] of the environment's expectations or contingencies fail to match adequately [Hawkins 1986], then planning an intervention that will reduce that mismatch. The task of treatment is to carry out that intervention, monitor progress, and make adjustments in the intervention as suggested by the results obtained through the monitoring.

The intervention can take one or more of three directions. It can address the youngster's behavior directly, the obvious and frequent strategy already discussed. It can address the environment's demands and expectations. And, it can address the environment's teaching and motivational character. These last two—the environment's demands and expectations, and the environment's teaching and motivational character—are often the cause of the mismatch between environment and behavior, and it is intervention in these ecological factors that is here called indirect. The literature on parent training [e.g., Dangel and Polster 1984; Graziano and Mooney 1984] is replete with examples in which a youngster's behavior was changed by such indirect intervention, such as when the parents were taught to interact differently with their child in order to teach and motivate behaviors that would better match parental expectations. Occasionally, there are clinical cases in which the child's behavior does not need to change, the only needed correction is in the environment's expectations [Hawkins 1986].

To the extent that a TFC program arranges for reasonable expectations and effective teaching and motivation in the youngster's biological family, school, and peer environments, that program belongs at the intensive end of the TFC continuum on the dimension of indirect intervention. Programs that do little or no intervention with the youngster's biological family, peers, or school environment belong at the least intensive end of the TFC continuum on the dimension of indirect, ecological intervention.

Support and Supervision of TFC Parents.   All TFC programs give more support and supervision than is found in foster family care. Elsewhere in this volume Snodgrass and Bryant report that although many TFC programs have client caseloads of ten or fewer per staff member, some report caseloads as high as 35 youngsters. This latter seems to fall well outside a range that could legitimately be said to provide a program of treatment. Even caseloads in the 16 to 20 range, which were found to be common, seem unlikely to provide effective individualized assessment and treatment to any but the most mildly disturbed, disturbing, or retarded youngsters, given the fact that the TFC parents are paraprofessionals, not mental health experts with years of training. In fact, Snodgrass and Bryant found that most TFC programs provide only four to six sessions of preservice training; more than ten sessions is quite rare. With such brief training for TFC parents, great reliance is placed on the potency and breadth of the support and supervision provided (often by persons of modest training themselves), otherwise effective treatment seems precluded.

Of course, the specific content of the support and supervision, not simply the caseload, is also a critical consideration. For example, some programs have systematic in-home training curricula for TFC parents, while many programs appear to have no planned inservice training of any kind, group or individual. All programs offer consultation and crisis assistance, but programs vary considerably in the extent to which staff members have, as the basis for most of this intervention, a standard, coherent technology based on clearly explicated principles. Programs no doubt also vary in the frequency, locus, medium, and content of their routine consultation or supervision of TFC homes. Some programs indicate that staff members are expected to meet with the TFC parents at least once a week [e.g., Larson et al. 1978], for as long as a half day each time [Freeman 1978], though this is a kind of process variable that should be measured regularly if one is to have confidence that it actually occurs as planned [cf. Hawkins et al. 1981, 1982]. Such a level of direct contact with the TFC family and client youngster seems appropriate for the more intensive end of this dimension, and of course would need to be combined with frequent indirect contact, by telephone and memorandum.

Another factor that is important but much harder to measure is the manner in which the TFC parent is treated by the staff. A style that conveys respect, appreciation, and the expectation that the parent will perform professionally appears to be quite powerful in promoting high-quality work [Freeman 1978; Hawkins et al. 1985].

A related factor, of course, is the level and type of remuneration of TFC parents. Some TFC developers seem to suggest that a salary promotes more professional performance from parents than does a per diem payment [Freeman 1978]. This remains to be evaluated experimentally. Another dimension that seems more certain to have an effect is the level of payment. If, in addition, the level of payment is based on systematic performance evaluations, parent motivation seems likely to be further enhanced.

One final cluster of factors that seem very important but are again difficult to specify and measure can be characterized as enthusiasm, energy, bias for action, optimism, resourcefulness, and commitment to getting results. These are the kinds of behaviors found by Peters and Waterman [1982] to typify unusually well-managed, productive corporations. Some of the specific staff behaviors involved are frequent positive interaction, positive feedback about performance, humor, and nondefensive sharing of problems and solutions. High levels of activity and unwillingness to give up on a problem are also components [Hawkins et al. 1985].

When TFC parents get high levels of support and supervision they will be more capable of providing an intensive treatment program than with lower levels of support and supervision.

Staff Selection and Training.   Regardless of the extent and content of TFC parent training, support, and supervision, TFC parents will not be able to do an effective job of treating very difficult youngsters if the staff members providing that training, support, and supervision are not well trained and experienced themselves.

In general, the higher the credentials required of staff members, the more potential the program has for intensive service. TFC would not be a relatively low-cost service, however, if the majority of the staff members had to be doctoral-level therapists. Many programs do require a master's degree, but the majority require only a bachelor's degree [see Snodgrass and Bryant, this volume].

Perhaps more important than formal credentials are the personal characteristics of staff members, their previous experience, and the training they receive from the agency. It may be that a program's potential is best facilitated by a staff that is of diverse professional background rather than all of one discipline or one level of training, so that various skills and bodies of knowledge can be drawn upon to address the myriad issues faced in a TFC program.

Regardless of their diverse backgrounds, however, staff members do need to be formally trained in the agency's approach, treatment technology (including when to apply a particular technique), and expectations. The Daly paper, elsewhere in this volume, illustrates such training. No previous professional training is adequate to prepare a staff member for the diverse problems of TFC, and even if it did, the person would still need to learn the particular approach and values of an agency if a well-coordinated system of treatment is to be implemented.

To the degree that a program selects skillful, experienced, energetic, and resourceful staff members of diverse previous training and experience, and then provides systematic training that adequately establishes the staff performance necessary to implement the intended program with fidelity, that program belongs at the intensive end of the TFC continuum in terms of staff selection and training.

Program Accountability.   This final dimension of program intensity has different meanings to different people, and it certainly is a multidimensional concept that cannot be fully described here. In general, it means that the program as a whole and its individual units are being held responsible for stating clearly what they will do and then for showing that they have done it. Accountability applies to all services, teams, and individuals. When accountability is defined this way it becomes evident that all levels of program evaluation are a part of accountability, in some sense.

In TFC, accountability includes such things as developing procedure manuals that tell what the intended program procedures are, measuring the fidelity with which those procedures are actually implemented, measuring other program characteristics for which there may be no particular plan, and measuring important outcomes of the program and its components. For example, a program can record its intended procedures and criteria for TFC parent recruitment, selection, training, support and supervision; client admission and matching of clients with TFC families; client assessment; treatment plan development and treatment procedures; progress assessment; discharge planning and execution; follow-through after discharge; staff recruitment, selection, training, support and supervision; biological family intervention; and so forth. This kind of thing is usually done in the form of manuals.

But writing the intended procedures does not assure their implementation. It is common for programs to say that they provide, for example, "close supervision" of TFC parents; but this is hardly more than a vague claim unless the supervision is defined in some measurable terms and then measured in actual practice. The fidelity of implementation of intended procedures is often far less than program directors and other representatives know, especially where implementation is difficult or not monitored by one's superiors. Measuring the fidelity of implementation would reduce such misinformation. In fact, it sometimes uncovers procedures that are being used but were not planned; some of these procedures turn out to be worth adding to the plan.

Other variables that are important to measure but are not usually part of any procedure manual are characteristics such as TFC parent demographics (age, education, family size, etc.), client demographics, rate of referrals, or client family demographics. These data can be useful in conducting small, in-house research projects addressing such questions as: "Are our single TFC parents as effective as our couples?" "What is the education level of our TFC parents?" "Are our master's-level staff members more successful than those on the bachelor's level?" "With what subgroups of youngsters are we most and least effective?"

Of course, client outcomes are the reason for the program's existence and must be measured. Ideally, a program would measure the problems of the youngster and biological family at the time of entry into the program; the degree of actual client contact and compliance with treatment procedures during the program; the positive and negative outcomes obtained while the youngster is in the program; the youngster's and biological family's status (in a habilitative, therapeutic sense) at the point of discharge; the positive and negative outcomes obtained during follow-through (if the program conducts it); and the outcomes several months or years later [Hawkins et al. 1981, 1982]. In actual practice, the expertise and financial resources available to most TFC programs will usually limit their measurement of outcomes to a few of these, but certainly some of them should be measured routinely.

One kind of inexpensive yet useful measurement is consumer satisfaction [cf. Wolf 1978]. The satisfaction of youngsters and their parents can be measured annually, for example, or the satisfaction of the referring agencies can be measured. Similarly, staff members' satisfaction with the performance of their supervisors and peers can be informative.

Finally, it should be pointed out that there are many different audiences and readerships that will take an interest in certain data on the program and its clientele. Depending on the particular data, potential audiences within an agency conducting a TFC program include: the board; the chief executive; any public relations persons; the program director; staff members who recruit, supervise, or train TFC parents; TFC parents; client families; and client youngsters. External to the agency, potential audiences include: the scientific and professional community; referral agencies; nonreferral funding sources; accrediting organizations; and the general public [cf. Hawkins et al. 1981, 1982].

To the extent that a TFC program holds itself accountable—by stating its intended procedures, measuring the implementation of those procedures, measuring other relevant program and client variables, measuring outcomes, and then reporting data to relevant audiences— that program belongs toward the intensive end of the TFC continuum on the accountability dimension.

Naming Points on the Continuum

Some TFC programs appear not to consider the TFC parents' role as including treatment [e.g., Barnes 1980]; others are sharply focused on active treatment [e.g., Hawkins et al. 1985], and most are probably between these extremes. This range of emphasis is the continuum just described.

It may be worth assigning different names to programs on this continuum. Those at the less intensive end of the continuum primarily emphasize caring for a special-needs youngster, so the popular term "specialized foster care" or "special foster care" seems applicable. "Intensive foster care" would be a third possibility. For programs at the more treatment-focused, intensive end of the continuum, a name is needed that clearly separates the service from regular foster family care, otherwise, outside professionals will not view the service as genuine treatment for severely disturbed, disturbing, or retarded youngsters. Similarly, legislators, mental health systems, and child welfare systems will underestimate the potential of the service as well as the need for adequate funding. While the term "treatment" (or therapy, habilitation, etc.) needs to be emphasized—such as by placing it last in the name for the service (like "driver" in "truck driver" or "instruction" in "skydiving instruction")—the fact that it is done primarily by persons in a parenting role and in a family living context needs to be communicated as well. This makes terms like "foster family-based treatment" [Hawkins et al. 1985], "foster family treatment" [Bryant et al. 1986], or "family-based treatment" [Hawkins and Luster 1982] appealing.

Whether it is worthwhile to attempt names for one or more points between the most treatment-focused end of the continuum and the least treatment-focused end is uncertain. What does seem certain is the need to acknowledge clearly the range of treatment focus included among programs that would identify themselves with TFC.

Potency, Breadth, and Restrictiveness of TFC and Other Services

Therapeutic services are of many kinds. The most familiar to the general public are probably outpatient, office-based counseling and inpatient psychiatric hospitalization. But in addition there are, of course, group homes, parent training, halfway houses, telephone crisis intervention, residential crisis intervention, residential treatment centers, intensive treatment units, and others.

Therapeutic services vary on three important dimensions that influence their effects and our society's current acceptance of them: treatment potency, breadth of treatment, and restrictiveness. The first two of these make up the more general dimension of treatment intensity mentioned earlier and are implicitly defined by the seven TFC dimensions already described, though not always as separate concepts, while restrictiveness has yet to be defined at all. A treatment program of any type can be located in a matrix of these three general dimensions, and thereby evaluated in terms of its potential for producing long-term, broad benefits to the client and its risk of producing at least short-term detriments or "costs."* The three dimensions will first be defined and then the matrix presented.**

Potency of Treatment. This refers to the power of an intervention to produce change in the specific behavior or behaviors targeted, as reflected by the speed and magnitude of that change. Most of the seven variables discussed earlier contribute to an overall TFC program's potency (though most also contribute to its breadth). To be more specific, variables that contribute greatly to potency include the functional relevance of the specific behaviors targeted for each individual; the quality of the relationship between TFC family members and the client youngster; the arrangement of other motivative operations that, like the interpersonal relationships, affect the potency of healthy and unhealthy reinforcers and punishers [cf. Hawkins 1986]; the clarity and consistency of rules, instructions, and suggestions; the objectivity and consistency of monitoring the youngster's behavior so that procedures are changed in a timely fashion; the immediacy of social, activity, and material consequences; and the potency of those consequences for the youngster.

It is possible for almost any treatment program to deliver potent individual treatment. Certainly an institution, group home, outpatient service, or TFC family has that capacity, at least in theory. Actual practice, however, often falls far short of that for many reasons, some theoretical and some systemic. In institutions, for example, the clients and the staff members are so separated from the normal, daily living for which the client needs to be prepared that realistic selection of target behaviors is greatly impeded. The staff members who have the most contact with the client are often not trained, monitored, or paid well enough to engage in constant, potent treatment. Further, clients are grouped and thus often teach maladaptive behaviors to one another.

*It would be more accurate and precise to speak of the nature of the programming provided for a particular youngster, rather than the nature of a program as a whole, but it would be less relevant to the purpose of this book.

**This analysis is adapted from Hawkins and Luster [1982].

In outpatient treatment the problem of staff separation from the client's natural environment is still present, but at least the client is in that environment almost all of the time. To the extent that clients are taught to be objective, precise observers and reporters of their own behaviors and the environmental events surrounding them, the professional has a chance of selecting relevant target behaviors and monitoring progress. If, in addition, the professional uses potent intervention procedures, as described earlier, potent treatment is likely.

In TFC we try to have most of the treatment carried out by the TFC family, especially the TFC parents. Of course, they rarely have the skills of a professionally trained therapist, which is why certain TFC program dimensions described earlier—such as TFC parent selection, training, supervision, and accountability—are so important. However, TFC parents do have the advantage of observing the youngster daily in the kinds of contexts where his or her problems exist, and the situations of daily life, so relevant targeting is facilitated.* They also have ample opportunity to create one of the most potent motivative variables: a positive (but firm and consistent) relationship with the youngster. And they have control over innumerable, potentially potent consequences: their approval or disapproval, their interest and appreciation, their joy and disappointment, many kinds of privileges and activities, edibles, playthings, games, trips, and so on. In spite of some serious limitations, TFC seems to hold the potential for truly potent treatment.

Breadth of Treatment.   This refers not to the potency of the procedures addressed to any particular behavior but to three other variables: the number of different situations in which the behavior is monitored and changed; the number of different, related behaviors and values changed, so that each becomes part of an interlocking cluster; and the number of different persons whose behavior is changed, so that the youngster's natural social ecology becomes more accepting and/or better at teaching and maintaining adaptive behavior. Examples of broad or systemic treatment include negotiating with the youngster's school principal to get the youngster special tutoring in a subject; getting a teacher to see how difficult the youngster's life has been and

---

*This is not completely accurate, because the TFC parents do not often see the youngster in his or her own family, neighborhood, and perhaps school. By contrast, intensive in-home intervention programs such as Homebuilders [Kinney et al. 1981; Kinney et al. 1977] do have this opportunity. But they give up some other advantages that TFC has.

therefore spend a minute each day in private, personal conversation with the youngster to establish a potent relationship; helping a youngster's single mother find an apartment in a neighborhood with few delinquent youths; teaching a father how to play with his son; teaching the youngster to make friends with peers who will be a better influence; teaching the youngster home-maintenance, consumerism, and other routine living skills; and helping the youngster get started in interests, hobbies, or sports that others will admire, such as fishing, model-building, jogging, tennis, crocheting, ping-pong, gardening, art, or baseball.

TFC is an ideal context for broad treatment. In fact, some degree of breadth is almost inevitable in family living, because the youngster is with family members so much of the time and they model, instruct, and give feedback on a wide variety of behaviors. A family is also likely to make at least some modest efforts to see that the youngster's school experience goes well, and may even offer some guidance to the youngster's biological parents. Few other treatment strategies have the potential for breadth that TFC does, the exceptions being home-based intervention and school intervention. Even most residential Re-Ed programs [Hobbs 1982], which put serious effort into changing the youngster's natural ecology, are limited by the fact that the youngster is not living in a family home. To achieve maximum breadth, a TFC program would need to make its ecological intervention systematic and extensive, as implied by several of the seven variables identified earlier.

Restrictiveness. The third dimension on which treatment programs (or individual programming) can be described is their restrictiveness. The restrictiveness of treatment and education environments has become an important legal consideration since *Lake v. Cameron* [1966] and *Wyatt v. Stickney* [1972] [Martin 1975]; but, unfortunately, the concept is rarely, if ever defined [MacMillan 1982: 11], even in writings focused on the subject of restrictiveness [e.g., Turnbull et al. 1981]. Nevertheless, definition is needed if the concept is to be used consistently and fairly.

To define restrictiveness adequately it is important to avoid confusing it unnecessarily with treatment potency and breadth. Although potent and broad treatment will often be more restrictive than less potent or broad treatment, this is not always the case; and it certainly is not the case that restrictive programs are necessarily more potent or broad. In fact, the most restrictive programs are often the least potent and nearly always the narrowest. There are at least five reasons: (1) the staff members who interact most with the client are often poorly selected, trained, supervised, or motivated, while the best-trained staff members insulate themselves from direct observation and intervention in the client's daily living; (2) the client is not living under the stimulus conditions of normal daily life and therefore does not exhibit some of the behavioral assets and liabilities that need to be assessed and addressed; (3) the staff members are typically so separated and insulated from the client's natural environment that intervention there is both difficult and not defined clearly as part of their role; (4) each client is typically grouped with other clients who promote deviant behavior that provoke staff members to focus their attention primarily on that behavior, even though it is only part of the client's problems and perhaps even a superficial part; and (5) it is so easy to manipulate a few simple but potent punishment and deprivation contingencies—such as locks, physical restraint, and denial of basic privileges (activity, social interaction, pleasant food, etc.)—that serious attention to the client's long-term benefits appears less necessary, sometimes even irrelevant.

A definition of restrictiveness should be phrased in measurable terms and should separate restrictiveness from treatment potency and breadth as much as possible, while still capturing its own relevant characteristics. Thus the definition should not imply that obvious interventions are necessarily more restrictive than subtle ones, that interventions that alter daily routines are necessarily more restrictive than ones that do not intrude into typical daily living, or that consistent and potent interventions are necessarily more restrictive than inconsistent or weak ones.

The essence of restrictiveness appears to involve three kinds of "cost" to the client. Most are short-term costs, and some can be used to help the client therapeutically and thus produce substantial long-term benefits. But restrictiveness is a short-term issue, while treatment is a long-term one.

The three costs are as follows: denial or impediment of access to the rewarding events that are available to others of similar age or developmental level; arrangement or provision of punishing events that are not normally experienced by others; and denial or impediment of access to habilitative learning experiences (a long-term cost). A fourth factor should be added, one that is related to all three of these costs: the duration and breadth of the cost. It should also be added that the denial or impediment of access to rewarding or habilitative experiences and the imposition of punishing experiences can be due to the planned rules and requirements of the program, to unplanned informal contingencies, or to the nature or location of the physical facility in which the program is carried out. Thus, the more a treatment program or physical facility does such things as isolate the client from peers, withhold meals, restrict the client's choice of clothing, permit social rejection of the client, put the client in embarrassing situations, require performance of unusual tasks, stigmatize the client, or separate the client from normal family and school experiences, the more restrictive it is. And the longer each of these costs is applied, the greater the restrictiveness. It should be obvious that the more institutional the program, the more restrictive it is. But it must also be recognized that any intensive (potent and/or broad) treatment will involve at least some degree of restrictiveness, even if that program is TFC or intensive home-based intervention.*

A Matrix Comparing Programs in Terms of Benefits and Costs to Clients. Figure 1 is a matrix based on the three dimensions just described: potency, breadth, and restrictiveness. Each dimension is arbitrarily divided into five levels, from least to most. To illustrate use of the matrix in terms of residential treatment programs for children and adolescents, a few examples of programs will be considered.

The typical state hospital placement for a youngster would probably be about a 1 in breadth, a 1 or 2 in potency, and a 5 in restrictiveness. This makes it easy to see, in graphic terms, why hospitalization is so vigorously opposed by many persons in the fields of mental health, child care, and law. By way of contrast, short-term hospitalization in a psychiatric facility that extensively involves the family in both assessment and treatment, provides potent and extensive skill training, includes substantial outreach to a youngster's school, and substantial follow-through after discharge, would probably be about a 3 or 4 in breadth, 4 or 5 in potency, and, because of the short duration (not the broad and potent treatment) only 3 or 4 in restrictiveness.

A typical group home that is located in a residential neighborhood, with the client youngsters attending public schools, would probably be a 3 in breadth—depending on such things as whether the group home parents maintained the property, prepared meals, and budgeted for

---

*A more comprehensive definition is available on request but is too long for inclusion here.

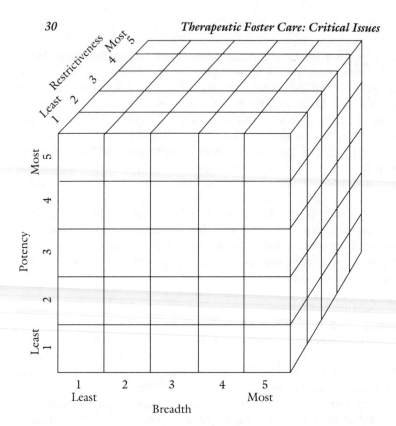

*Figure1—A matrix for describing or evaluating treatment program-
ming on two dimensions having to do with the likely effectiveness of
treatment—the potency of the procedures for changing the behaviors
or other variables targeted, and the breadth of such targeting—
and one dimension of "cost" to the client (at least in the
short run), restrictiveness.*

themselves, and on whether youngsters were involved in such activities—a 1 or 2 in potency, and a 2 or 3 in restrictiveness. By contrast,
a group home like Teaching Family Model homes [Blase et al. 1984]—
in which youngsters live with the same couple continuously (instead of
shift staff) and potent, broad training of each youngster is provided
[e.g., Minkin et al. 1976]—would probably qualify for a 4 in breadth
and a 5 in potency, though still a 2 or 3 in restrictiveness.

A typical residential treatment center with self-contained schooling
would probably be about a 2 in breadth, a 3 in potency, and a 4 in
restrictiveness. By extensive involvement with the youngster's natural

ecology, potent training on numerous individually selected skills—selected at least partly in a constructional, systemic way [Goldiamond 1974, 1984; Hawkins 1986]—and effective reintegration of the youngster into his or her natural school and home environments, such a treatment center might become a 3 or 4 in breadth, a 4 or 5 in potency, and only a 3 in restrictiveness.

Now consider regular foster family care, specialized foster care, and foster family-based treatment. Because these take place in the routines of normal family, school, and neighborhood living, they are almost necessarily at least 4 in breadth. If the youngster's functioning in his or her school and biological family are observed and modified as needed, the breadth would probably be 5. Although most regular foster family care is probably only 1 in potency, most TFC programs probably range from 2 to 3 at present. Programs like PRYDE (described briefly in Hawkins et al. 1985) are striving to achieve a consistent potency of 4 or even 5, though this may prove unattainable within practical limits of funding, TFC parent selection, TFC parent training and supervision, staff selection, and so on. Finally, in terms of restrictiveness, TFC programs and regular foster family care probably belong in the 1 to 2 range. The restrictiveness is not a simple 1 because the youngster is not usually in a permanent family context; and more intensive programs will tend to be somewhat more restrictive than the less intensive because the former are likely to make privileges and other reinforcers contingent upon performance of certain behaviors, require the youngster to get involved in prosocial interests whether or not he or she initially wishes to, and so on.

It is also instructive to consider even less restrictive programs than TFC, but ones that are clearly a form of treatment. For example, typical once-a-week counseling for a youngster would be a 1 in restrictiveness. For most youngsters, however, it probably is also only a 2 or 3 in potency and a 2 or 3 in breadth. It could be made highly potent by the use of techniques that have been experimentally demonstrated to produce major, rapid changes and by documenting such changes objectively, so that it could become a 5 in potency. It could also be made broader, but only if the clinician ventures into the youngster's natural ecology for assessment and intervention. Office-based parent training would also be only a 1 or 2 in restrictiveness, 3 to 5 in potency, and 2 to 4 in breadth, all depending on the context and method. Intensive home-based intervention would be about 1 in restrictiveness, 3 to 5 in potency, and 5 in breadth. TFC personnel would be well advised to observe the advantages of such intervention and, as Friedman suggests elsewhere in this volume, consider whether some of the youngsters they serve could not be even better served in such a program.

It is tempting to suggest that any treatment program can be evaluated by adding its scores on the two positive dimensions—breadth and potency—and subtracting its restrictiveness score. Programs with higher remainders would always be preferred, if they were appropriate for the particular type of client. However, these three scales are without basis in research and would have to be matched in terms of comparability of intervals. At any rate, the matrix provokes consideration of the implications of various kinds of programming for youngsters and of ways that the seven dimensions described earlier might be used to improve the potency or breadth of existing programs.

Conclusions

TFC is a fairly new development with many roots and a promising future. Depending on local needs and resources, it appears capable of considerable potency, and it is intrinsically fairly broad in scope and minimal in restrictiveness. With energetic, informed, creative program development; extensive research and evaluation; and generous sharing of proven technologies, the full potential of TFC can be achieved.

REFERENCES

American Psychiatric Association. 1987. *Diagnostic and statistical manual of mental disorders* (3rd ed.) (rev.). Washington, DC: American Psychiatric Association.

Barlow, D. H.; Hayes, S. C.; and Nelson R. O. 1984. *The scientist practitioner: Research and accountability in clinical and educational settings.* New York: Pergamon.

Barnes, K. 1980. *Individualized model for specialized foster care for "hard to place" juvenile offenders.* Washington, DC: The National Center on Institutions and Alternatives.

Blase, K.; Fixsen, D.; and Phillips, E. 1984. Residential treatment for troubled children: Developing service delivery systems. In *Human services that work: From innovation to standard practice,* 149–165, edited by S. C. Paine, G. T. Bellamy, and B. L. Wilcox. Baltimore, MD: Paul H. Brookes.

Braukmann, C. J.; Ramp, K. K.; and Wolf, M. M. 1980. *Progress report for Achievement Place: Phase IV*. Lawrence, KS: Achievement Place Research Project.

———; ———; Tigner, D. M.; and Wolf, M. M. 1984. The Teaching-Family approach to training group-home parents: Training procedures, validation research, and outcome findings. In *Parent training: Foundations of research and practice*, edited by R. F. Dangel and R. A. Polster. New York: Guilford.

Bryant, B. 1980. *Special foster care: A history and rationale*. Verona, VA: People Places, Inc.

———; Snodgrass, R. D.; Houff, J. K.; Kidd, J.; and Campbell, P. 1986. *The Parenting Skills Training*. Staunton, VA: People Places, Inc.

Catania, A. C., and Bringham, T. A. 1978. *Handbook of applied behavior analysis: Social and instructional processes*. New York: Irvington.

Cochran, D. C., and Shearer, D. E. 1984. The Portage Model for home teaching. In *Human services that work: From innovation to standard practice*, 93–115, edited by S. C. Paine, G. T. Bellamy, and B. L. Wilcox. Baltimore, MD: Paul H. Brookes.

Dangel, R. F., and Polster, R. A., eds. 1984. *Parent training: Foundations of research and practice*. New York: Guilford Press.

———, and ———. 1988. *Teaching child management skills*. New York: Pergamon.

De Fries, C.; Jenkins, S.; and Williams, E. C. 1970. Foster family care for disturbed children: A nonsentimental view: In *Child welfare services: A sourcebook*, 193–209, edited by A. Kadushin. London: MacMillan.

Dinkmeyer, D., and McKay, G. 1973. *Raising a responsible child*. New York: Simon and Schuster.

Dreikurs, R. 1957. *Psychology in the classroom*. New York: Harper and Row.

Fabry, B. D.; Almeida, C.; Hawkins, R. P.; Fabry, P. L.; and Weaver, P. M. 1987a. *A system for collecting follow-up information on youths discharged from PRYDE: A therapeutic foster care program*. Poster presented at the Association for Advancement of Behavior Therapy convention, Boston, MA.

———; Meadowcroft, P.; Frost, S. S.; Hawkins, R. P.; and Conaway, R. L. 1987b. Low cost, high validity, multiuse data: Practical program evaluation in a family-based treatment program. In *Evaluating behaviors/agencies in community settings: Successes and future directions*, chaired by D. W. Wesch. Symposium presented at the Association for Behavior Analysis convention, Nashville, TN.

Fanshel, D., and Shinn, E. B. 1978. *Children in foster care: A longitudinal investigation*. New York: Columbia University Press.

Fixsen, D. L.; Phillips, E. L.; and Wolf, M. M. 1973. Achievement Place: Experiments in self-government with pre-delinquents. *Journal of Applied Behavior Analysis* 6: 31–47.

Freeman, H. 1978. Foster home care for mentally retarded children: Can it work? *Child Welfare* 57: 113–121.

Goldiamond, I. 1974. Toward a constructional approach to social problems: Ethical and constitutional issues raised by applied behavior analysis. *Behaviorism* 2: 1–85.

————. 1984. Training parent trainers and ethicists in nonlinear analysis of behavior. In *Parent training: Foundations of research and practice,* 504–546, edited by R. J. Dangel and R. A. Polster. New York: Guilford.

Gordon, T. 1970. *Parent effectiveness training: The tested way to raise responsible children.* New York: Peter H. Wyden.

Graziano, A. M., and Mooney, K. C. 1984. *Children and behavior therapy.* New York: Aldine.

Hawkins, R. P. Developing potent behavior-change technologies: An invitation to cognitive behavior therapists. *The Behavior Therapist.* (In press.)

————. 1986. Selection of target behaviors. In *Conceptual foundations of behavioral assessment,* 331–385, edited by R. O. Nelson and S. C. Hayes. New York: Guilford.

————; Fremouw, W. J.; and Reitz, A. L. 1981. A model for use in designing or describing evaluations of mental health or educational intervention programs. *Behavioral Assessment:* 307–324.

————; ————; and ————. 1982. A model useful in designing or describing evaluations of planned interventions in mental health. In *Practical program evaluation methods in youth treatment,* edited by A. J. McSweeney, W. J. Fremouw, and R. P. Hawkins. Springfield, IL: Charles C. Thomas.

————, and Luster, W. C. 1982. Family-based treatment: A minimally restrictive alternative with special promise. In *Behavioral treatment of youth in professional foster homes,* chaired by E. L. Phillips. Symposium presented at the American Psychological Association convention, Washington, DC.

————; Meadowcroft, P.; Stark, L. J.; Trout, B. A.; and Grealish, E. M. 1982. Use of daily home data for monitoring treatment in PRYDE. In *Youth treatment in the "natural" environment: The developing foster family-based alternatives,* chaired by R. P. Hawkins. Invited symposium presented at the Association for Behavior Analysis convention, Milwaukee, WI.

————; ————; Trout, B. A.; and Luster, W. C. 1985. Foster family-based treatment. *Journal of Clinical Child Psychology* 14: 220–228.

————; Peterson, R. F.; Schweid, E.; and Bijou, S. W. 1966. Behavior therapy in the home: Amelioration of problem parent-child relations with the parent in a therapeutic role. *Journal of Experimental Child Psychology* 4: 99–107.

Hobbs, N. 1966. Helping disturbed children: Psychological and ecological strategies. *American Psychologist* 21: 1105–1115.

———. 1982. *The troubled and troubling child: Reeducation in mental health, education, and human service programs for children and youth.* San Francisco: Jossey-Bass.

Hoier, T. S., and Cone, J. D. 1987. Target selection of social skills for children: The template-matching procedure. *Behavior Modification* 11: 137–163.

Kelly, J. 1983. *Solving your child's behavior problems: An everyday guide for parents.* Boston, MA: Little, Brown and Company.

Kinney, J.; Haapala, D.; and Gast, J. E. 1981. Assessment of families in crisis. In *Treating families in the home: An alternative to placement,* 50–67, edited by M. Bryce and J. C. Lloyd. Springfield, IL: Charles C. Thomas.

———; Madsen, B.; Fleming, T.; and Haapala, D. A. 1977. Homebuilders: Keeping families together. *Journal of Consulting and Clinical Psychology* 45: 667–673.

Knitzer, J. 1982. *Unclaimed children: The failure of public responsibility to children and adolescents in need of mental health services.* Washington, DC: Children's Defense Fund.

Lake v. Cameron, 364 F.2d 657 (D.C. 1966).

Larson, G.; Allison, J.; and Johnston, E. 1978. Alberta Parent Counselors: A community treatment program for disturbed youths. *Child Welfare* 57: 47–52.

Lutzker, J. R. 1984. Project 12-Ways: Treating child abuse and neglect from an ecobehavioral perspective. In *Parent training: Foundation of research and practice,* 260–297, edited by R. F. Dangel and R. A. Polster. New York: Guilford.

MacMillan, D. L. 1982. *Mental retardation in school and society.* 2nd ed. Boston, MA: Little, Brown and Company.

Martin, R. 1975. *Legal challenges to behavior modification: Trends in schools, corrections, and mental health.* Champaign, IL: Research Press.

Martin, G., and Pear, J. 1988. *Behavior modification: What it is and how to do it.* 3rd ed. Englewood Cliffs, NJ: Prentice-Hall.

McSweeney, A. J.; Fremouw, W. J.; and Hawkins, R. P., eds. 1982. *Practical program evaluation methods in youth treatment.* Springfield, IL: Charles C. Thomas.

Minkin, N.; Braukman, C. J.; Minkin, B. L.; Timbers, G. D.; Timbers, B. J.; Fixsen, D. L.; Phillips, E. L.; and Wolf, M. M. 1976. The social validation and training of conversation skills. *Journal of Applied Behavior Analysis* 9: 127–140.

O'Dell, S. 1974. Training parents in behavior modification: A review. *Psychological Bulletin* 81: 418–433.

Pardeck, J. T. 1982. *The forgotten child: A study of the stability and continuity of foster care*. Washington, DC: Children's Bureau.

Patterson, G. R.; McNeal, S. A.; Hawkins, N.; and Phelps, R. 1967. Reprogramming the social environment. *Journal of Child Psychology and Psychiatry* 8: 181–195.

Peters, T. J., and Waterman, R. H. 1982. *In search of excellence: Lessons from America's best-run companies*. New York: Warner Books.

Stokes, T. F., and Baer, D. M. 1977. An implicit technology of generalization. *Journal of Applied Behavior Analysis* 10: 349–367.

Stroul, B. A., and Friedman, R. M. 1986. *A system of care for severely emotionally disturbed children and youth*. Washington, DC: CASSP Technical Assistance Center, Georgetown University Child Development Center.

Turnbull, H. R., III; Ellis, J. W.; Boggs, E. M.; Brooks, P. O.; and Biklen, D. P. 1981. *The least restrictive alternative: Principles and practices*. Washington, DC: American Association on Mental Deficiency, Inc.

Ullmann, L., and Krasner, L. 1975. *A psychological approach to abnormal behavior*. 2nd ed. Englewood Cliffs, NJ: Prentice-Hall.

Wahler, R. G.; Winkel, G. H.; Peterson, R. F.; and Morrison, D. C. 1965. Mothers as behavior therapists for their own chidren. *Behavior Research and Therapy* 3: 113–124.

———. 1980. The insular mother: Her problems in parent-child treatment. *Journal of Applied Behavior Analysis* 13: 207–219.

Watson, E. W.; Maloney, D. M.; Brooks, L. E.; Blase, K. A.; and Collins, L. B. 1980. *Teaching-Family bibliography*. Boys' Town, NE: Father Flannagan's Boys Home.

Weaver, P. M. 1987a. *A system for collecting follow-up information on youths discharged from PRYDE: A therapeutic foster care program*. Poster presented at the Association for Advancement of Behavior Therapy convention, Boston, MA.

Webb, D. B. 1988. Specialized foster care as an alternative therapeutic out-of-home placement model. *Journal of Clinical Child Psychology* 17: 34–43.

Williams, C. D. 1959. The elimination of tantrum behavior by extinction procedures. *Journal of Abnormal and Social Psychology* 59: 269.

Wolf, M. M. 1978. Social validity: The case for subjective measurement or how applied behavior analysis is finding its heart. Journal of Applied Behavior Analysis 11: 203–214.

Wyatt v. Stickney, 325 F. Supp. 781 (M.D. Alabama 1972).

Therapeutic Foster Care:
A National Program Survey

ROBERT D. SNODGRASS
BRAD BRYANT

S INCE THE EARLY 1950s, and increasingly in recent years, a model of specialized foster family care has been developing that is aimed at meeting the needs of children who require the intensity of structure typically provided in institutional programs, but who could benefit from the richness and normalizing influence of a true family environment. Variously termed Special Foster Care (SFC) and Foster Family-Based Treatment (FFBT), these programs, with all their variety, are presently encompassed under the designation Therapeutic Foster Care (TFC). They are linked conceptually by their use of the foster family setting, their common focus on exceptional children, and their common historical relationship to the movement for deinstitutionalization of handicapped citizens requiring supportive or therapeutic services [Bryant 1980]. Since little had been done to identify the broad parameters of TFC programs generally, although such a "big picture" certainly would lend coherence to their continuing evolution, a survey was undertaken of as many programs as possible that identified themselves as special foster care, foster family-based treatment, or similar name.

Method

A nine-page questionnaire was designed to yield numerical and brief narrative information on six topics: program identification, client

37

information, specialized foster parent information, foster parent support services, treatment planning, and funding. The instrument itself contained 71 items, most of which were either open-ended or multiple choice. Questionnaires were sent in March and April of 1984 to 129 agencies in the United States and Canada. Many of these agencies had responded to a 1980 mail survey of SFC/FFBT programs in the 50 states and two Canadian provinces, to identify existing TFC programs and to assess their characteristics. Over 220 programs were located at that time and responses were obtained from more than 100. The current questionnaire was sent to these 100 and to 29 others located since 1980 through various contacts and publications. This appears to be the most extensive survey to date of such programs.

Results and Discussion

Of the 129 questionnaires mailed, 48 were fully or partially completed and returned, a return rate of 37%. Responses included programs from 24 states and all major regions of the United States, as well as the Canadian province of Ontario. Forty-four programs reported a 1983 year-end census figure. Taken together, these 44 were serving a client population of 1,804 children. The size of subsamples providing data on particular survey items, however, varied somewhat, as will be seen in the following results.

With regard to organizational type, 12 respondents (25%) were public agencies. Four of these were local departments of social services, one was a local juvenile court service unit, and seven were state departments of human services. The remaining 36 programs (75%) were voluntary (nonprofit) agencies. There were no private, for-profit agencies in the sample.

Program Identification

Dates of Origin. Table 1 shows the identification numbers of respondents (identified in the appendix) listed in rows according to the date each made its first placement, and in columns according to the type of organization it represents. Five of the 48 respondent programs did not provide data regarding their first placement.

The conspicuous absence of programs begun before 1970 may be the result partly of the sampling procedures employed; current pro-

TABLE 1—TFC PROGRAMS* LISTED BY TYPE OF ORGANIZATION
AND DATE OF FIRST PLACEMENT

| | Organization | | | | | |
| | Public | | | Private | | |
Date	Social Service	Mental health	Correct-ions	Social Service	Mental Health	Correct-ions
1970				-12-		
1971				-10-		
1972						
1973	-9-			-13-43-		
1974				-21-		
Sub-Totals:	(1)			(5)		(6)
1975				-14-	-39-	
1976				-16-40-	-25-	
1977	-36-			-4-33-		
1978	-18-24- -27-			-15-28- -34-45-	-20-23-	
1979	-37-			-22-29- -42-	-1-26- -48-	
Sub-Totals:	(5)			(12)	(7)	(24)
1980	-44-			-41-	-8-46-	
1981	-5-		-38-	-35-	-3-	
1982				-31-32-		
1983	-19-					
1984				-7-47-		
Sub-Totals:	(3)		(1)	(6)	(3)	(13)
TOTALS	(9)	(0)	(1)	(23)	(10)	(0) (43)

*Programs are listed by their identifying number (see appendix) grams begun before 1970 may well exist. Bryant [1980], however, identified a number of promising programs from the late 1960s that did not survive due to the short-term funding arrangements for such experimental programming, which may help to explain the relatively low number of early programs reporting current data.

Type of Organization. Voluntary programs have predominated throughout the period represented. In our sample only one program from the early 1970s was state operated. Programs sponsored by mental health agencies appear to have begun operations primarily during the latter half of the decade, and most of them seem to be voluntary. Despite the probable oversampling of late 1970s programs—due to an emphasis on program needs in the 1980 survey and thus perhaps a larger return rate from newer programs—the data suggest an increasing rate of new program development over time. The number of TFC programs begun in the first half of the 1980s is more than double the number begun in the first half of the 1970s, even with very limited representation for 1984. However, the fact that the sampling method ruled out locating programs that had opened and then closed again before this survey makes it impossible to be conclusive about rates of new program development.

While voluntary programs continue to predominate through all periods, the future may see a change. The authors have seen a marked increase recently in the number of requests for training and consultation in TFC program development from local public welfare agencies.

Of the 36 voluntary programs in the sample, 10 (28%) are operated by community mental health centers, which are a product of the deinstitutionalization movement and community mental health legislation of the early 1970s, and which are often so dependent on public agencies for their origination and continued funding that they are functionally somewhere between public and private. Though tied most closely to mental health agencies, many of these programs work directly with local departments of social services. Some are licensed as child-placing agencies. All of the remaining 26 programs are tied closely to departments of social services both as a source of referrals and for regulatory oversight. Twenty-four (92%) of these are licensed child-placing agencies.

Few voluntary programs (9%) reported taking legal custody of the children they serve, although those licensed as child-placing agencies are authorized to do so if they choose. All public programs, however, did report taking custody of their clients. Public agencies, of course, are legally mandated and funded to assume guardianship of children whose biological parents are unable or unfit to provide care. Where custody directly affects programming, as in cases where a child moves into permanent care in a voluntary program's special foster home, the provider agency must work closely with the custody agency for the long-term welfare of the child.

Service Area.   Half of the programs sampled (50%) accept statewide referrals. The remaining programs were divided about evenly between those serving children on a regional, multicounty basis (29%) and those restricting service to a more limited local area (21%). In some cases, it is clear that the service area is related to population density: programs in large metropolitan locations can maintain an acceptable client census while serving a narrower geographic area. To remain viable in less populous locales, programs may need to serve a larger area to bring about sufficient client referrals.

Program Purpose.   There was considerable agreement among responses to the item asking agencies to describe the major purpose of their TFC progams. Of the 46 respondents, 31 (67%) identified the provision of a family alternative to institutional placement as at least one major purpose. This focus reflects the historical trend toward deinstitutionalization, the increasing difficulty of getting public money for expensive institutional programs, and an increased appreciation for the value of family life. A third of the respondents (33%) described their programs as providing an alternative to regular foster family care, while others (22%) were seen as transitional programs serving children leaving institutions with the goal of returning home. Some respondents (13%) emphasized the term "treatment" in characterizing their agency's purpose. Less frequent responses included the provision of emergency shelter (9%), long-term care (7%), supplementary services supporting the agency's residential treatment center program (2%), and preparation for adoption (2%). Given the frequency of multiple responses (41% or 19 of 46 respondents), it appears that many agencies do not have a single focus or purpose and that it is not unusual for programs to serve a range of purposes for children.

Two of the responding programs indicated that they provide short-term emergency shelter services only. Data from these programs are not included in subsequent tables and discussions.

Client Information.   Statistical information on the children and adolescents served in the programs in 1983 was limited to a single year to provide data usable for comparisons. Open-ended questions were included that sought to identify characteristics of children served and not served.

1983 Client Census.   The 39 programs reporting usable client census data were serving a total of 1,344 children and adolescents at the close of 1983, for an average of 35 youngsters per program. Figure 1

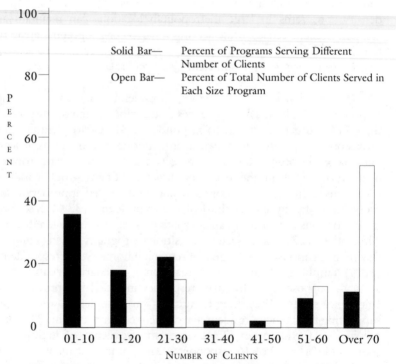

*Figure 1—Percentage of TFC Programs and Clients as a
Function of Program Size, 1983*

gives a breakdown of program size. The solid bars represent percentages of programs serving different numbers of clients, while the open bars indicate what percentage of the total number of clients were served in each size of program.

The range in program size was striking. While the most frequent census total was 10 clients, the largest agency reported a 1983 closing census of 320. Over one-third of the programs served no more than 10 clients each, but only about 8% of all the children in the sample were served in these small programs. The majority of programs (77%) worked with 30 clients or fewer, yet the majority of clients were served in the four large programs of 70 or more. These figures would appear to underscore the importance of careful oversight and evaluation procedures, given that poor service by a single large program would have a broad negative impact on special-needs children in a particular service area.

A final observation may be of particular interest to new programs or those currently involved in program planning. Of the 17 programs with a client census of more than 20, only one began operating since 1980. It would appear that the process of building a census typically requires some time to accomplish.

Sex, Race, Age. Data on sex, race, and age of TFC clients are presented jointly with similar data from a study of children in all forms of foster care done for the federal Children's Bureau in 1977 by the Westat Corporation [Shyne and Schroeder 1978]. Although there are important technical differences between the two studies with regard to sample size and methodology, the findings at least suggest significant contrasts between regular and special foster care client populations.

In the Westat sample, 59% of the children were black, 32% white, and 9% of other racial/ethnic backgrounds. The majority of the children (63%) were preadolescent. Although the racial composition of the two sample groups was roughly similar, the TFC sample showed a higher proportion of white children (67%) and a lower proportion of both black (28%) and other (5%) children. The TFC sample also contained a somewhat higher proportion of males (62% vs. 53%) than did foster family care generally. This is in keeping with the general finding that behavior disorders are more commonly diagnosed among boys [Knopf 1979].

The distribution of client ages in the TFC programs surveyed was rather narrow. Of the 39 programs providing age information, 28 (72%) reported average ages from 12 to 15 years. One program with a census of five reported an average age below nine years and only two reported average ages above 15. The overall mean age for all TFC programs was 12.8 (s.d. = 2.25), and the modal age was 14.

Age data offer the most dramatic quantitative difference between regular foster care and TFC populations. As mentioned earlier, only 37% of the foster children in the Westat study were between the ages of 13 and 17 years, but in the TFC sample nearly two-thirds of the children (62%) fell in this range. Any direct comparison between regular foster care and TFC should take this age difference into account. Certainly an important part of the explanation is the fact that a sizable proportion of children in TFC have experienced previous foster care placements and are likely to have been in the child welfare system for a relatively longer period of time.

1983 Admissions and Discharges: Indications of Growth.   Thirty-nine agencies reported a total of 834 admissions and 558 discharges for 1983. Individual programs admitted anywhere from 0 to 263 children during the year, while, in most cases (67%), the number of discharges for particular agencies was 10 or fewer children. The discharge distribution was large, extending from 0 to 121.

Admission and discharge figures parallel the census data reported in figure 1. A small number of programs account for a large proportion of the totals. For example, 35 of the smaller programs together admitted a total of 385 children in 1983, while the remaining four admitted 449 clients, or 54% of the total. Similarly, the 36 smaller programs together discharged 194 children in 1983, while the remaining three discharged 264, or 47% of the total.

In the aggregate, the foregoing programs grew by 276 children in 1983 (total admissions minus total discharges). The number of clients served by individual programs generally increased as well. Twenty-four (64%) of the 39 programs reported growth, which ranged from one child to 142. Eleven agencies (28%) reported small declines in census, ranging between one and five clients. Three agencies (8%) reported no change in total census in 1983. In sum, the proportion and rate of census decline is consistently small, while the rate of increase in some cases is high. These data suggest that the model is growing not only in terms of number of new programs, as discussed earlier, but also with regard to the number of clients served collectively and individually by the agencies reporting here.

Preadmission Placements. Respondents were asked to specify the placement each child was in immediately preceding admission to their TFC program. Although the information could not supply the full scope of these clients' preadmission experience, it was felt that many respondents would find it difficult or impossible to provide detailed preplacement histories with any accuracy. Immediate preplacement information could prove useful to a discussion of the appropriate use of the TFC model in the continuum of available residential options, and also could throw light on the population of children served in TFC. Another concern here was the extent to which children enter TFC as their first out-of-home placement, since a major purpose of the model is to offer a family-based alternative to more restrictive residential settings.

Thirty-four agencies provided information regarding preadmission placements for clients admitted and/or discharged in 1983. Table 2 shows both the placements from which children entered the 34 programs and the placement to which children were discharged from these programs in 1983. Those entering from less restrictive settings in general ranged from 0% to 100% in individual programs. The wide variation among TFC programs with regard to the relative proportions of children admitted from more or less restrictive settings may reflect the difficulty of the client populations served by different programs.

In only 32% of the cases was TFC used as a placement option for children removed from their biological families. This does not mean that these children had never been removed from their families before their placement in TFC, or that they had not experienced more restrictive placements previously. The "prior placements" identified in table 2 simply may represent the most recent in a series of placements that include, for example, a return to the biological home before admission to TFC. More typically, the programs appear to serve children who have experienced multiple and often more restrictive placements previously. This should not be surprising, given that most early TFC programs appear to have been designed explicitly as transitional settings for children leaving residential treatment [Bryant 1980]. TFC care also is not as widely available or as well known as the more restrictive group home and residential treatment settings. Over the long term, TFC

TABLE 2—CLIENT ADMISSIONS AND DISCHARGES LISTED BY THE
RESTRICTIVENESS OF THEIR PRE- AND POST-TFC PLACEMENTS

Admissions		*Discharges*	
Less Restrictive Prior Placements	Percent	Less Restrictive Post Placements	Percent
Biological Family or Relative	32%	Biological Family or Relative	41%
Adoptive Family	02%	Adoptive Family	06%
Regular Foster Home	18%	Regular Foster Home	18%
		Independent Living	14%
Total	**52%**	**Total**	**77%**
More Restrictive Prior Placements			
Group Home	13%		
Residential Treatment Center	19%		
Detention	08%		
Other	08%		
Total	**48%** **N=487**		

programs may move toward serving as earlier, more diversionary alternatives for children who must leave less restrictive environments.

Postdischarge Placements.　　One fundamental measure of a program's success is the extent to which it is able to return children to less restrictive settings when they leave. Respondents were asked to identify the number of children who entered less restrictive settings immediately following discharge from their programs in 1983. As with preadmission data, postdischarge information is limited in that it does not indicate whether the client remained in the first post-TFC setting or experienced further placements later on. Immediate postdischarge data, however, are at least suggestive of outcomes. They also have the obvious advantage of eliciting a higher frequency of survey responses than would be expected if extensive follow-up information were requested. There are two examples, at least, of more complete follow-up studies conducted by programs operating in the 1970s [Larson and Allison 1977; Snodgrass and Campbell 1981].

Table 2 presents a breakdown of 1983 postdischarge placements of 383 children. Three-fourths (77%) were discharged to less restrictive settings and thus may be considered to have been diverted from group home or institutional care, at least in the short term. More significantly, perhaps, no agency reported placing fewer than 50% of discharged children in less restrictive settings, with the exception of one program whose only discharged child in 1983 went on to a more restrictive placement.

Of those children discharged to less restrictive settings, two out of five (41%) returned to their own or to a relative's home, 16% went to independent-living arrangements, and 6% were adopted. These latter two categories have particular significance in that they suggest both the potential of the TFC models to provide permanence and the need for such programs to build in ancillary services with regard to adoption and training for independent living.

Diversion from Group Homes and Institutions. The survey data do not allow a full assessment of the impact TFC programs may have on the diversion of their child clients from more restrictive residential settings. A comparison between the number of children entering TFC from less restrictive settings with the number of children leaving TFC to less restrictive placements, however, does suggest a positive impact generally on diversion.

Since the children that respondents reported as admitted and discharged in 1983 are not, for the most part, the same children, only loose comparisons between the two groups are possible, and then only if it is assumed that the populations are sufficiently similar. Table 2 shows that a greater proportion of children (77%) left TFC programs to less restrictive circumstances than entered from such settings (52%). Insofar as the foregoing assumptions and qualifications have validity, the TFC programs have diverted many children from more restrictive placements.

Length-of-Stay Data and Policies.   For the 34 reporting agencies, the average length of stay of children discharged in 1983 was 14.12 months (s.d. = 10.45, median = 11.50, mode = 12), ranging from a low of three months to a high of 54 months. The variation appears to relate principally to individual programs' purposes and to whether permanent placement with a foster family is allowed. Some programs, for example, are designed principally for short-term treatment while others seek to provide long-term or permanent placements.

Only four of the 46 agencies providing information on their length-of-stay policies reported a predetermined maximum tenure in care; it ranged from three to 24 months. That so few programs impose length-of-stay limits indicates that unlike group home and institutional programs, TFC may be adapted to the long-range placement needs of clients. Permanence is possible, within the broad model, for children who cannot return home. Nearly three-quarters (73%) of the sampled programs indicated that permanent placement was possible with their families even if it resulted in a transfer of the supervision to another agency and the subsequent permanent loss to the TFC program of a space in that home.

Children Admitted and Not Admitted to TFC.   Although the foregoing preadmission placement histories and demographic information offer some indication as to the nature of the population served in TFC, respondents also were asked to provide a brief narrative description of the children they serve. Probably no agency served an unmixed or unidimensional client population. This should not be surprising since there is no standardized notion at this point as to just what TFC should do and for whom. The multiple family environment of TFC permits serving a wide range of problems concurrently [Hawkins and Luster 1982]. Given sufficient numbers of competent families, the potential chief population that may be served in TFC clearly is quite broad.

Forty-one (91%) of 45 agencies reported serving at least some children with mild to severe emotional/behavioral disorders and 24 (53%) identified this population as their primary focus. These are the types of problems that traditionally tend to disrupt regular foster care placements [Pardeck 1982]. For 18 (40%) of the programs, severe emotional disturbance is the primary focus and may be characteristic of all the children they serve. Twenty-three agencies (51%) work with disturbed clients, as well as with one or more other types of disorder including physical handicaps, mental retardation, and the somewhat vague category of "hard-to-place" children that includes sibling groups. Four of the respondent agencies (9%) specialize in serving children with handicaps other than emotional or behavioral, such as mental retardation and/or physical handicaps. Eight agencies (18%) reported no particular specialization and indicated they would work with any handicapping condition.

Although emotional and behavioral disturbances were cited most frequently as presenting problems, only half of the programs (51%) reported serving only a single population such as emotional/behavioral disorders, physical handicaps, or mental retardation. Among programs serving more than one population, 48% listed two or more populations they would serve, 26% listed three or more, and 2% listed four. It was rare to find examples of handicapping conditions never served by TFC programs at some time. Children have been placed who are autistic or actively psychotic. Some children have been served in TFC who could not be served successfully in group homes or institutional programs [Bryant 1984].

There are, of course, limitations to the kinds of problems TFC programs can handle in any great numbers. It is unlikely that any of the respondents in this study would claim that TFC could or should replace the institution completely. Despite strong commitments to minimally restrictive, community-based programming, all in fact indicated that there are clients they will not accept, a tacit acknowledgment of the potential negative impact on the communities and on foster families of children whose problems present a serious threat to themselves and others. Specifically, 22 of the 43 programs (51%) would reject an applicant who had a history of dangerous behavior, although programs differed as to what constituted such behavior. Nearly half of the respondents (47%) would reject a drug-dependent child. One out of three programs (37%) would reject children diagnosed as psychotic and children for whom fire-setting is a presenting problem. Others identified less frequently as inappropriate for TFC were children who represent a sexual threat to other children (5), chronic law violators (3), suicidal children (3), children for whom no biological family members were available as resources (1), and children not legally free for adoption (1). Some of these distinctions clearly relate to individual program purposes rather than to the inherent capacity of the TFC model itself.

There are, of course, some intrinsic limits to the service capacity of a community and of a foster family-based program. The availability of appropriate families, the tolerance of neighbors, the range of staff expertise, and pressures on community resources, particularly the schools, all may militate against or for a child's acceptance by a particular program. Agencies that include supportive services such as special education programs, institutional components, or specialized staff members often are able to serve children with more serious disorders. Therapeutic foster care programs, however, are not secure facilities by design or intent and cannot offer the degree of client or community protection provided by most of the more restrictive placement settings, even though they may often be more habilitative for the client.

Special Foster Parent Information

The role of the "special" or "professional" or "treatment" foster parent clearly is central to the TFC model. Respondents were asked to provide demographic information on their foster parents and to describe the method they used to recruit, select, train, and evaluate them. These topics are likely to be of particular interest to new program planners. It is the authors' experience in assisting new programs that recruitment tends to be the paramount concern of program developers. Quality services clearly depend on the recruitment of the most competent families available. It would be a mistake, however, to assume that the development of a successful TFC program is simply a matter of finding sufficient numbers of "super foster parents." Most foster parents need effective training and technical support from TFC agencies on a continuing, intensive basis in order to deliver the quality care and programming of which they are capable. All program elements must be given equal consideration if an effective service is to be developed.

Thirty-five agencies reported a total of 900 foster families approved for special-needs children. Most of these families (85%) currently had one or more children in their homes, the mean being 1.3 (s.d. = .48); some 15%, then, were in reserve. That latter proportion, along with an unknown number of vacancies in homes where foster parents were authorized to serve more children than currently placed, reflected the degree of choice the agencies had in selecting families for newly admitted children or those requiring re-placement. As in traditional foster care, the need for additional families represents an ongoing and often urgent concern among TFC staff members. More than one-third of the agencies (37%) reporting, in fact, indicated that all their foster families were in use at the close of 1983. Although agencies do try to avoid keeping trained families waiting for placement, having to use all available families makes preplacement visiting for new children or moving a current child difficult.

Recruitment.   The recruitment and selection of TFC foster parents is not unlike the process involved in filling an important staff position. An agency needs to have a clear sense of what the foster parent will be asked to do, what population of potential applicants is most likely to have the necessary competence and interest in the job, and, finally, how this population can best be reached.

Respondents were asked to describe their recruitment approaches. Of the 42 programs reporting, 93% included word of mouth as a useful method and 69% identified it as their single most productive strategy. Because it depends, however, on an existing cadre of quality families, word of mouth is not a useful strategy with which to launch a program, although there are important implications here for new program developers. Since word of mouth recruitment relies on foster family satisfaction with agency services, the approach is only as good as an agency's perceived quality of support to parents. In beginning and maintaining a quality TFC program, program developers would be wise to select and support the first few families with particular care, given the long-term impact these families may have in recruitment [Hawkins et al. 1985].

Nearly half of the respondents (45%) reported using the classified ad section of local newspapers. Other media frequently used included public service radio (36%) and television announcements (24%), presentations to church and civic groups (31%), and direct mailings (10%). Several additional strategies were mentioned by one or more programs: (1) the use of qualified regular foster parents as TFC parents (primarily by public agencies); (2) an emphasis on face-to-face personal contacts with potential applicants; (3) the use of church publications, adult education announcements, library information centers, and school newsletters; (4) the development of a regular recruitment committee composed of staff members and foster parents; and (5) employment of a full-time professional recruiter.

Selection.   Respondents were asked if they employed qualification requirements for foster parent applicants beyond the state standards under which they operate. All 44 programs responding to this item had added to state standards the completion of preservice training. Nearly two-thirds (64%) did not, as a rule, allow placement of children before completion of the training. Besides attendance at training, two programs required satisfactory performance by participants on homework assignments, quizzes, or role plays before they were eligible to serve children in the program.

Beyond the preservice training requirement, there was no general agreement among programs on specific selection criteria. With regard to formal education, two agencies stated a preference for college graduates, one agency required the primary caretaker to have a bachelor's degree, and one program required foster parents to have completed high school. Two programs reported that they use only married couples as foster parents, and one program required single parents to identify a teammate who could provide support and occasional relief.

With regard to age criteria, four programs specified a minimum age of 21, two set the minimum at 25, and two gave 60 as the maximum age. Experience was another selection variable for some programs. Seven programs mentioned the importance of previous experience, and five specified kinds and amounts of experience for approval. Distance was noted as a selection variable by three programs, one of which required foster parents to live within 70 miles of the office. Another required foster parents to reside in the same community as the child's biological family.

Several other selection requirements were identified. Positive personal references were mentioned by some. Others required that one foster parent be home full-time. One program reported not using families receiving public assistance. Three programs required formal assessments such as psychiatric evaluation, the MMPI, the McCauley Questionnaire and Behavioral Test. One program stipulated an interview with the agency board of directors.

Preservice Training.   Preservice training is useful in several ways. It provides an opportunity to acquaint applicants with the agency and with the nature of their task as TFC parents. Specific skills such as behavior management techniques, observation and assessment methods, or self-help training can be presented and rehearsed. It also provides the agency with a sample of current behavior suggestive of applicants' interest, competence, and potential commitment. Attendance, promptness, participation, completion of homework, and understanding of particular content show indirectly what may be expected of applicants later on. Initial training, in fact, appears to have particular value as a selection mechanism by which applicants often screen themselves out by simply not meeting attendance requirements. From observations presented by Snodgrass [1977], it would appear that at least three preservice sessions for potential foster parents may be needed from which to predict adequately an applicant's commitment to the task of becoming fully trained.

Of the programs surveyed, 32 were able to provide specific information concerning their training requirements. Figure 2 shows the number of preservice sessions offered by these programs. Two agencies require a single preservice session, usually combined with the social worker's home study visit, and one agency reported requiring 14 preservice sessions. Aside from these extremes, most agencies require four to six sessions, the average being 5.84 (s.d. = 2.68).

In the analysis of responses concerning preservice training content, descriptions of topics covered were used to differentiate agencies whose focus appeared to be primarily knowledge oriented from those that included a skills orientation as well. A knowledge orientation was reflected by emphasis on the presentation of information to participants. Such topics as Stages in Child Development, Legal Aspects of Foster Parenting, or The Foster Child's Experience were considered to represent knowledge-oriented content. The preservice training curricula of 19 programs (56%) were classified as knowledge oriented.

A skill orientation involved emphasizing actual behavior that participants were to demonstrate as foster parents. Topic areas such as Behavior Management Skills and Communication Skills were considered to be skill oriented and such topics were emphasized by 15 programs (44%).

It was thought that training content might be influenced in part by the nature of the children served. A second type of grouping therefore was made. Agencies that appeared to primarily serve severely emotionally/behaviorally disturbed children were treated as one group (n = 13); programs whose clients appeared to generally present only

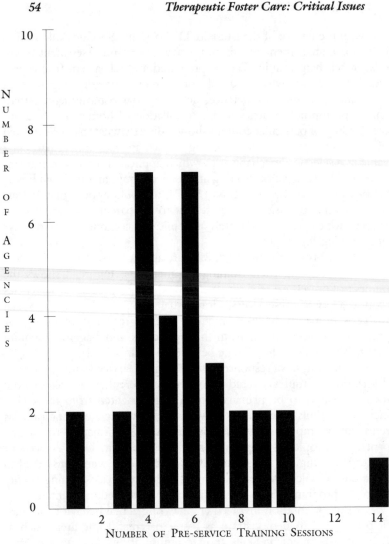

*Figure 2—Number of Preservice Training Sessions
Provided by TFC Programs*

mild to moderate emotional/behavioral disorders, physical handicaps, or mental retardation alone were taken as a second group (n = 21).

Among the 13 programs serving more severely disturbed children, two out of three (69%) reported some skill orientation in preservice; 31% did not. The proportions were reversed for the 21 programs serving mildly disturbed clients or clients with other handicaps: nearly three-quarters (71%) reported a knowledge orientation, while 29% reported some skill training as well. Although these figures are based on somewhat subjective classifications of training content and primary client populations, they do suggest interesting and understandable differences in preservice training orientation between programs serving more and less severely disturbed children.

The majority of programs (52%) reported providing orientation to agency policy and expectations in their preservice training. Two agencies employed an adaptation of the Teaching Family Model training for group home parents [Wolf et al. 1972]. Others used the Child Welfare League of America's or NOVA University's curricula for training foster parents in the regular foster care system. Training methods ranged from lectures through practicum experiences that emphasized role plays and direct experience. One agency reported providing a $10 incentive payment to each couple for each training session.

General Foster Parent Characteristics. Respondents were asked to describe the population of foster parents with which they work in terms of income, education, age, and other basic demographic information. Twenty-nine agencies provided average ages of foster parents, but some responses were only estimates. All programs reported average ages ranging between 30 and 45. Within programs, foster parents ranged in age from 20s to early 70s.

Only 19 agencies were able to provide information on income. Program averages ranged quite widely, from $9,000 to $25,000 annually, while individual foster families ranged from a subsistence level (represented by foster parents dependent on AFDC payments) to an upper-middle income level of $50,000. It is not known whether income averages differ between the populations of special and regular foster parents, but one study that compared these two groups on several demographic variables reported a slight, nonsignificant income difference favoring TFC parents [Hampson 1975]. No other demographic differences were found in this study; the two populations were distinguished, however, with regard to measures of parental skill and contingency management, again favoring the TFC parents.

As might be expected, income averages correlated somewhat with average years of education. Of 31 respondents, 52% reported the average level of foster parent education as completion of high school. One-third of the respondent programs (35%) reported an average level of foster parent education as high school plus some college or other advanced training. Two agencies indicated an average of less than high school completion, and two reported an average at the B.A. level.

Matching Children to TFC Parents. Respondents were asked what factors weighed most in their decision to place a particular child with a particular family. In regular foster care, emphasis traditionally has been placed on families' stated preferences regarding children's age, sex, and life circumstances. Therapeutic Foster Care programs sampled in this study consider family preference important. Of 34 reporting, 74% mentioned family preference as significant in making placement decisions. It should be noted that preferences can and do change with experience, and that agencies may be wise to exercise caution in basing matching decisions on families' initial preferences only.

In addition to family preference and the number and ages of children already in the home, respondents reported using a number of other criteria. Forty-seven percent sought to match the child to a foster family with proven skill for dealing with the problem. Perseverance with particular problems was a major criterion for 35%. Such assessments, of course, can only be made after a foster family has been in service for some time. Other decision factors included the desirability of placing siblings together (44%), consideration of a foster family's cultural similarity to the child's background (38%), the foster family's proximity to the biological family (21%), and the child's preference for an urban or rural setting (15%).

Much of the research concerning this very important decision in child placement has searched, without definitive results, for the characteristics of good or perhaps super foster parents [Snodgrass and Campbell 1979]. As mentioned earlier, superparents who can work well with most children and with only minimal supervision are a rare breed. Far more common are foster parents who will work well with certain children if given considerable support and direction from the agency. It may be true that no amount of support will compensate for a very poor match between child and foster parents, and that a very good match at times may require only minimal consultation to sustain the placement. These extremes, however, represent the exception, not the rule. Most placements fall somewhere between. An adequate and balanced emphasis on both matching and support is necessary to achieve a successful placement. Unfortunately, current understanding of what constitutes effective practice in these two areas is far from complete.

Foster Parent Support Services

Probably no service distinguishes TFC programs more clearly than the nature of the supervision and technical assistance given their foster parents. Respondents were asked several questions regarding their supportive services in an effort to identify any differences or similarities among them. One of the factors that may reflect the capacity of an agency to provide intensive, responsive support services is the size of the maximum caseload carried by a single direct-service worker.

Caseloads.   Table 3 shows the number of programs with various maximum caseload sizes. In the 29 agencies responding, the average maximum was 15.17 (s.d. = 9.33), with the range being two to 35 children. Most (79%) reported maximum caseloads of 20 children or fewer. Some of the considerable variation among programs on this dimension may relate to the client population served. For ten programs serving more severely disturbed clients, the average caseload maximum was 12.5 (range = 5–25). Those 15 programs serving moderately disturbed children averaged a maximum caseload size of 17.3 (range = 2–35).

The Case Manager.   The agency staff member directly responsible to families and children obviously has a key role in any TFC program. Whether the title is caseworker, social worker, case manager,

TABLE 3—NUMBER OF PROGRAMS REPORTING VARIOUS MAXIMUM
CASELOAD SIZES IN TFC PROGRAMS

| *Maximum Caseload* | *Other Responsibilities?* | | *Total* |
Size (# children)	*Yes*	*No*	*Programs*
01–05	3	—	3
06–10	10	—	10
11–15	3	2	5
16–20	3	2	5
21–25	2	1	3
26–30	—	—	—
31–35	1	2	3
Totals	**22**	**7**	**29**

foster parent supervisor, or program manager, the direct service responsibilities are roughly the same. Although state licensing regulations may set educational requirements for this position, 29 of 44 programs (66%) reporting require the case manager to have at least a bachelor's degree, while the remaining 34% require a master's degree. Many programs stressed the importance of relevant direct experience as a further qualification.

As table 3 indicates, case managers in most programs (76%) are required to perform additional duties beyond direct supervisory and supportive services to foster families, biological families, and children. Their responsibilities may include foster parent recruitment, preservice training, child counseling, casework with non-TFC children, representing the child in court, maintaining compliance with licensing standards, intake work, consultation to schools, coordination of services with other agencies, discharge planning and follow-through, and program evaluation. There would appear to be a relationship between maximum caseload size and the extent of a case manager's responsibilities. All agencies reporting caseload maximums of 12 children or fewer, for example, require case managers to perform additional functions beyond direct casework. In such instances, overall program quality would seem highly dependent on the broad competence of a few key staff members since they carry out the bulk of the program's entire work load.

Inservice Parent Training and Evaluation.   In addition to more traditional casework activities, the case manager in TFC serves as a trainer and consultant to foster parents. This distinctive role is reflected in the fact that nearly all respondents included individualized, child-specific training of the foster parents in the foster home as a major component of their inservice training program. In at least two programs, specific programmed curricula were used by case managers in these home-based sessions.

Half of the respondents (50%) indicated that they offer more formal inservice foster parent training on a regular basis. Some sessions are designed primarily to serve social or emotional support-group functions; other sessions focus on teaching specific parenting or treatment-related skills. Other programs offer no formal inservice training but suggest readings and community workshops for foster parents to attend and sometimes subsidize tuition for college courses related to their parenting tasks. Most agencies appear to blend inservice foster parent training with regular casework service regardless of the number or nature of additional formal meetings scheduled.

The majority of programs (68%) reported that they formally and regularly evaluate foster parent performance. Typically, the evaluations are done annually in connection with recertification of the home or more often, as required by state licensing standards. Some programs reported undertaking a "debriefing" of foster parents following each terminated placement as part of their family evaluation-feedback process. Information generally was not provided on the specific nature of formal evaluations, although much of it appears likely to be governed by the dictates of state licensing standards.

Case Manager Supervisors.   All 34 agencies reporting indicated that they provide case managers with regular supervision. Nearly all supervisors (94%) have master's or doctoral degrees, 65% of which are in social work. As with case managers, respondents stressed the importance of relevant experience as a fundamental prerequisite for supervisory staff. Academic backgrounds may be more reflective of state requirements than of agency preference or professional orientation. Supervisors were reported to consult with case managers at intervals ranging from daily to monthly.

Treatment Planning

The information collected in this study does not provide the basis for a clear distinction between "treatment" and "nontreatment" special foster care programming, although differences among agencies in degree and design of treatment-oriented intervention are suggested. The data do indicate, however, that TFC programs typically assume responsibility for producing, maintaining, and tracking change in clients regardless of how they define "change" goals or the methods they employ to achieve them. This fundamental responsibility for change is one thing that makes TFC different from traditional foster family care and what likens it in some ways to more traditional residential treatment models. Agencies were asked to provide information concerning their treatment or change procedures, beginning with the intake information they require for admission, through their client assessment and their approaches to discharge planning.

Intake Requirements.   There was little variation among programs with regard to the information and documents they required concerning the child before admission. Most programs required a psychological evaluation, social history, and educational and medical records. A majority of the 43 agencies reporting (79%) also required or encouraged preplacement visits between the child and the prospective foster family. For some programs, these visits may occur during the interview process. For others, separate visits in the prospective home are arranged. A few agencies required that special preplacement behavioral inventories be completed. Several programs required psychiatric evaluations before admission.

Treatment Planning.   Of 45 respondents, four out of five (82%) indicated that they maintain a written treatment plan on each child in care. Examples of treatment goals typically defined in these plans ranged from remediation of specific behavioral problems, through modification of children's attitudes, to the teaching of developmental self-help skills. Goal definitions appear to be related both to the client population served and to the agency's theoretical orientation to the treatment process. Plans are designed in most cases by agency staff members, although outside experts occasionally are used. Typically, treatment plans are formally updated two to four times a year.

The case manager generally appears to assume responsibility for seeing that plans are carried out, and foster parents take primary responsibility for direct implementation. These are the explicit role assignments for 69% of the respondent programs. For a few agencies, foster parents are characterized as providing support to the psychologist or other therapist who, in turn, provides treatment to the child. It is not clear in these cases that foster parents' responsibilities are different from those of foster parents in regular foster care. For the most part, however, TFC appears to represent a practical extension of theoretical principles favoring the family as the primary treatment setting for children [Alexander and Parsons 1973; Hawkins et al. 1966].

Related Services.   Early TFC programs frequently were developed as ancillary, aftercare services to supplement traditional residential treatment programs. Some contemporary TFC agencies supplement their own programs with ancillary services of various kinds. One important example is the agency-operated special education program for more seriously disturbed youngsters. It enables the TFC agency to work with children otherwise not suitable for community placement due to the lack of appropriate public school resources, and to provide greater continuity between the treatment programs implemented at the foster home and the school. Special-education services also provide a much needed backup in situations where a child is not performing acceptably in public school.

Twenty-eight respondent agencies identified a number of additional programs supplementary to TFC itself. Among them were individual and/or group family counseling (61%), afterschool programs (26%), and private tutoring (14%). Also mentioned were summer camps, day and weekend summer recreation programs, nursery schools, and respite care programs to relieve foster parents. Related services like these allow further structuring of the child's time and ease the pressure agency staff members typically experience when much of the child's program depends upon outside community resources and voluntary supports, which often are not willing to persevere with particularly disturbed and disturbing youngsters.

Treatment, Assessment, and Follow-up. All 42 agencies responding to questions regarding evaluation of clients' treatment progress indicated that they do some sort of in-program assessment. All reported making regular subjective reviews of client change. Many (43%) also undertake more objective measures, typically in the form of frequency data or other written observations recorded by foster parents. Formal testing also is employed, although to a lesser degree (12%).

Few TFC agencies appear to be collecting regular follow-up information on the children they discharge from their programs. Of 41 agencies reporting, 17 (41%) indicated that they do no follow-up evaluations of children once they leave the program. For most of the remainder, follow-up consists of occasional, informal contact with some discharged children. One agency reported mailing follow-up questionnaires at regular intervals. Another reported being in the process of conducting a ten-year follow-up study. Some short-term follow-up data from TFC programs do exist and generally are favorable with regard to sustained positive outcomes for children [Fabry et al. 1987; Snodgrass and Campbell 1981; Larson and Allison 1977]. Both the Fabry et al. and Snodgrass and Campbell studies showed that more than 75% of the children followed were living in settings less restrictive than the TFC program from which they had been discharged.

Services to Biological Families. Respondents appeared to recognize the important role a TFC program can play in aiding a client's successful return to the biological family. Of 41 agencies providing information, four out of five (85%) provide services of some kind to biological families, varying broadly in type and intensity. Some agencies were just "available on request" to biological parents, and some simply provided help in arranging home visits. Most respondents (58%) offer counseling or family therapy to biological families. A third (34%) provide casework services, and 24% offer parenting training.

The degree and type of services TFC agencies offer biological parents may relate directly to the way TFC has been used as a placement option. Up to the present time, the model often has been employed as a placement of last resort, frequently after many and more restrictive placements already have occurred and parental rights have been terminated. Where TFC is used as an earlier option, as with children leaving their own homes for the first time, the goal of returning home is usually realistic, and services supporting it take high priority. As a family model, TFC would appear to have significant potential as a resource for the biological parents as well as the children. This is a direction that TFC programs are likely to take increasingly in the future.

Program Funding and Payment to Foster Families

Respondents were asked to provide information on their funding sources, operating costs, and payments to foster families. They also described any start-up resources used for program planning and development.

Only 24% of the 42 programs responding had obtained special funding for planning and development efforts. For those receiving such assistance, planning periods ranged from one to three years. Of particular interest was the report that three programs devoted a considerable portion of start-up time not to direct program planning but to efforts aimed at satisfying state licensure requirements.

The great majority of programs (93%) were funded through state or local public agency contracts or service grants that, in turn, derive largely from federal programs such as Title XX. Only one program was funded entirely by private foundation support, and one reported 90% funding through direct charitable contributions. Four reported receiving supplemental assistance from endowments or foundations. Typically, however, voluntary TFC programs operate by contract on some type of fee for service basis. Such arrangements, of course, leave them vulnerable to political decisions regarding federal and state expenditures and require frequent administrative adjustments to the shifting demands of public bureaucratic oversight.

Payments to Special Foster Parents. Figure 3 shows TFC programs distributed by the monthly amount paid in 1983 to their foster parents. Although payments were higher in every case than rates paid to regular foster parents locally, they ranged widely from a low of $185 to a high of $1,450 per month per child. With 42 agencies providing cost data, the average monthly payment to foster parents was $516.61 (s.d. = 241.38) and the median, $455.50.

The amount an agency decides to pay a foster family to provide TFC services logically will depend upon a number of factors, including local income averages, market conditions, and funding resources in general. Some programs reported varying individual fees depending on such factors as the foster child's age, severity of the handicapping condition, results of foster parent evaluations, level of foster parenting experience, and in at least one case, whether a particular placement is considered an emergency or not. One program reported making a portion of the monthly fees contingent upon foster parents' meeting specific task requirements such as timely submission of recorded observations on the child's behavior. Two agencies reported that they compensate parents less for the second child placed than for the first, which should discourage pressure from foster parents for placing a second child for income reasons alone.

Program Costs. Total program costs per child vary from $7,000 to $38,960 annually. Figure 4 shows these figures translated to a per diem basis. For the 31 programs reporting, the per diem range was from $19.18 to $106.74. The average per diem cost was $37.69 ($13,757 yearly), the median, $32.88 (s.d. = 20.22).

Thirty programs reported both total annual costs and payments to foster parents. The proportion of total per diem costs going to family per diem payments averaged 47%, ranging from a low of 17% to a high of 75%. On the average, nearly 50% of total program costs typically were paid to foster families. Sufficient information was not obtained to account for the wide variation in costs. Some undoubtedly must be due to the nature and number of ancillary services provided in addition to core special foster care services.

All programs reporting cost data stated that their costs were no

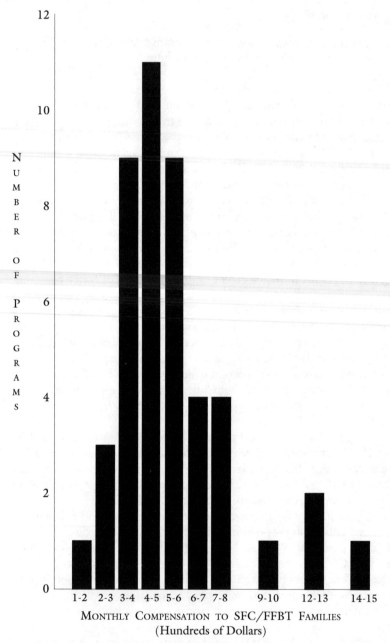

MONTHLY COMPENSATION TO SFC/FFBT FAMILIES
(Hundreds of Dollars)

Figure 3—Amount Compensated Foster Families by TFC Programs

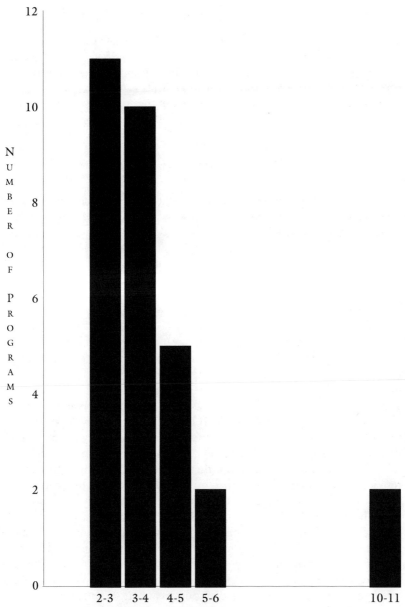

*Figure 4—Per Diem Costs of Special Foster Care Foster
Family-Based Treatment Programs*

greater than and, in most cases (92%), considerably less than the cost of alternative group home or institutional programs in their states. This is consistent with other comparative data indicating TFC to be the least costly of all out-of-home treatment models [Bryant 1984]. The economy of the model, of course, has been one of the advantages recognized since TFC programs began in the early 1950s.

General Discussion

The foregoing information on current TFC programs has been presented not from the perspective of how TFC should be done, but rather to characterize what in fact is being done by as large a sample of active programs as could be obtained. What biases exist in the sample are difficult to estimate. It seems likely that the very smallest, least established, or least well-managed programs would be less likely to be known to us or, if known, to return the survey. The sample may be biased toward better-managed, larger, and longer-established programs.

Having begun typically as an amplification of regular foster care or as a supplementary aftercare component of residential treatment centers, TFC programs appear to be employed increasingly as a full alternative to institutional placement for disturbed and disturbing children, and for other handicapped children as well. Programs operating today still reflect the spectrum represented by the historical development of the model. Some still function as ancillary, weekend services for residential centers and some still serve a treatment aftercare purpose, but most of those surveyed present themselves as alternatives to more restrictive placement settings and thus represent what is likely to be a trend toward the increased use of the model for that purpose.

Therapeutic foster care programs have clear advantages as placement options. They fill existing gaps in services to children who typically fail to achieve stability in regular foster care and therefore may be placed unnecessarily in group home or institutional settings. Unlike more restrictive placements, TFC allows for care and treatment in a true family environment. It is unique among treatment-oriented programs in its capacity to provide permanence, and the cost advantages can be enormous.

Beyond simply maintaining difficult children in care, these programs assume responsiblity for planned client change—for implementing treatment or developmental plans in the home. Super foster parents who can persevere with difficult children with little or no supervision are not typical of TFC parents or practice. Foster parents in the more accountable programs take on a quasi-staff function, receiving skill training, intensive oversight, and technical assistance, as well as emotional support. Paralleling qualitative changes in the role of foster parents are corresponding changes in the role of the case manager. In TFC programs that function as alternatives to more restrictive care, case managers serve as indirect providers as well as coordinators of services. In addition to emotional and logistical support, they offer individualized training and consultation to treatment foster parents regarding specific change strategies or treatment plans.

What of the future of TFC? If the indicators mentioned earlier hold true, we can expect to see a continuing expansion of the model in coming years, particularly as a service to children who currently tend to be placed in group homes or residential centers for the moderately emotionally disturbed.

The future of TFC is tied to other developments in the fields of child welfare and mental health, from which it originates. If the current emphasis on legal permanence in child placement continues, the future may see a significant decrease in traditional, temporary foster family care as children are maintained more effectively in their own families [Kinney et al. 1977; Maybanks and Bryce 1979] or freed for adoption. Should this occur, it may be that TFC services will come to be used far more frequently as a first out-of-home placement for disturbed children who have been maintained for prolonged periods in pathological family systems that simply could not be salvaged despite intensive professional support and intervention. It is not difficult to conceive of a continuum of family-based services combining support and training to biological families with TFC when needed.

Voluntary programs appear to dominate current TFC practice. In the future, however, as the availability of well-tested and articulated models grow, it is likely that more public sector programs will emerge. Some of the potential for public sector expansion, however, will be contingent on the degree to which public agencies can achieve small caseloads, in part by relieving workers from an overweight of paperwork. There is no substitute for effective and intensive training, support, and supervision services to foster parents providing TFC. Simply increasing payments to foster parents alone will not ensure a successful program, as has been demonstrated in more than one case [North

Carolina Division of Youth Services 1979]. With regard to organizational obstacles to public sector programming, however, action may be needed at the state and federal levels, as well as locally, to ensure that sufficient staff time is available to provide the direct support services so central to the model.

If public TFC programming does in fact expand, with that expansion will come a need for close coordination and cooperation between the two provider authorities: community mental health and public welfare. The territorial frictions and lack of coordination that too often characterize relations between the two fields will need to be overcome as professionals from both disciplines team together to create a type of treatment service that is highly dependent on consistency and coordination.

As TFC treatment develops and expands, the technology of the model can be expected to evolve as well. Given the fact that many children appear to continue in these programs until maturity, there will be a growing need for practical curricula and training materials, designed for use by foster parents and/or staff, covering such areas as prevocational skills, job-finding, and independent-living skills. Self-paced, competency-based skill-training and structured learning experiences would be most helpful as supplements to the individualized treatment/teaching plans developed by case managers and foster parents for implementation in the family setting.

It may be that TFC has even broader potential as a generic human services delivery model than is currently recognized. Although it has been used primarily as a treatment resource for children, variations of the model have been employed with adults as an aftercare service for recovering alcoholics, for recently discharged psychiatric patients, and for longer-term service to retarded adults. As the postwar baby boom generation moves toward old age and presents demands for increased resources, geriatric applications of the model are likely to become widespread as well. With the large-scale sectoral shifts from manufacturing to service anticipated in the coming decades, manpower will be increasingly available for in-home services of this kind, the growth of which are likely to be driven also by their relative cost-efficiency [Bell 1968; Henderson 1979; Naisbitt 1982].

Such longer-term conjectures notwithstanding, perhaps the greatest future impact of TFC will be on the traditional foster care system itself. As permanency planning efforts succeed in preventing out-of-home placements for more children, those children who do eventually enter foster care are likely to be older and more difficult to manage due to the longer periods they spend in pathological family situations while efforts are made to keep the family intact. Increasingly, regular foster care will need to serve a therapeutic purpose. Just as special education helped improve instruction in general education in the seventies and eighties, TFC may well influence the evolution of all foster family care in the years to come. That influence may be felt most strongly with regard to the roles of foster parents and case managers. Both are likely to assume more proactive functions in the future, with case managers increasingly taking on the role of in-home trainer/consultant and foster parents increasingly performing consciously as teachers and agents of adaptive change in children. While TFC clearly is a discrete program type with clear differences from traditional foster care, in some areas it may represent an advance in foster family service rather than a strict departure. As such, its relevance for all neglected and dependent children should emerge forcefully in child welfare practice.

REFERENCES

Alexander, J. F., and Parsons, B. V. 1973. Short-term behavioral intervention with delinquent families: Impact on family process and recidivism. *Journal of Abnormal Psychology* 81: 219–225.

Bell, D., ed. 1968. *Toward the year 2000.* Boston: Houghton Mifflin.

Bryant, B. 1980. *Special foster care: A history and rationale.* Verona, VA: People Places.

———. 1984. *Special Foster Care: Evaluation of an alternative to institutions for disturbed children.* Unpublished master's thesis, University of Virginia.

Fabry, B. D.; Meadowcroft, P.; Frost, S. S.; Hawkins, R. P.; and Conaway, R. L. 1987. Low-cost, high validity, multi-use data: Practical program evaluation in a family-based treatment program. In *Evaluating behavioral agencies in community settings: Successes and future directions,* chaired by D. W. Wesch. Symposium presented at the Association for Behavior Analysis convention, Nashville, TN.

Hampson, R. 1975. *Selecting and training foster parents as therapists: Community care for handicapped children.* Unpublished master's thesis, University of Virginia.

Hawkins, R. P., and Luster, W. C. 1982. Family-based treatment: A minimally restrictive alternative with special promise. In *Behavioral treatment of youth in professional foster homes,* chaired by E. L. Phillips. Symposium presented at the American Psychological Association convention, Washington, DC.

———; Meadowcroft, P.; Trout, B.A.; and Luster, W. C. 1985. Foster family-based treatment. *Journal of Clinical Child Psychology* 14: 220–228.

———; Peterson, R. F.; Schweid, E.; and Bijou, S. W. 1966. Behavior therapy in the home: Amelioration of problem parent-child relations with the parent in a therapeutic role. *Journal of Experimental Child Psychology* 4: 99–107.

Henderson, H. 1979. Redeploying corporate resources toward new priorities. In *Business in 1990,* edited by A. Starchild. Seattle, WA: University Press of the Pacific.

Kinney, J. M.; Madsen, B.; Fleming, T.; and Haapala, D. A. 1977. Home-builders: Keeping families together. *Journal of Clinical and Consulting Psychology* 45: 667–673.

Knopf, I. J. 1979. *Childhood psychopathology: A developmental approach.* Englewood Cliffs, NJ: Prentice-Hall.

Larson, G., and Allison, J. 1977. *Parent counsellors: Evaluation—outcome.* Alberta: Alberta Social Services and Community Health.

Maybanks, S., and Bryce, M., eds. 1979. *Home-based services for children and families.* Springfield, IL: Charles C. Thomas.

Naisbitt, J. 1982. *Megatrends: Ten new directions transforming our lives.* New York: Warner Books.

North Carolina Division of Youth Services. 1979. What they need is love: Second annual report on community-based alternatives in North Carolina. North Carolina DYS.

Pardeck, J. T. 1982. *The forgotten child: A study of the stability and continuity of foster care.* Washington DC.: University Press of America.

Shyne, A. W., and Schroeder, A. G. 1978. *National study of social services to children and their families.* Washington, DC: Children's Bureau.

Snodgrass, R. D. 1977. *Specialized foster care: A model for serving handicapped children.* Paper presented to the convention of the Virginia State Federation Council for Exceptional Children, Roanoke, VA.

———, and Campbell, P. 1979. *Computer-assisted matching of special-needs children with teaching "foster" parents.* Paper presented at the Virginia State Federation Council for Exceptional Children, Roanoke, VA.

———, and ———. 1981. *Specialized foster care: A community alternative to institutional placement.* Paper presented to the Association for the Advancement of Behavior Therapy, Toronto.

Wolf, M. M.; Phillips, E. L.; and Fixsen, D. L. 1972. The teaching family: A new model for the treatment of deviant child behavior in the community. In *First Symposium on behavior modification in Mexico.* Edited by S. W. Bijou and L. Ribies-Inesta. New York: Academic Press.

Appendix

Agencies (and individuals) responding to survey questionnaire listed alphabetically by state

1. *East Arkansas Region Mental Health Center*
   (Bert Strauss)
   Director, Substitute Care
   305 Valley Drive
   Helena, AR 72342

2. *Elizabeth Mitchell Childrens' Center*
   (Kay Kimbrough)
   6601 West 12th Street
   Little Rock, AR 72206

3. *South West Arkansas Counseling*
   (Randy K. White)
   P.O. Box 1987
   Texarkana, AR 75504

4. *Children's Garden*
   (Merrie Fanshel)
   Program Coordinator
   #7 Mt. Lessen Drive, St. B 256
   San Rafael, CA 94903

5. *San Francisco Department of Social Services*
   (Martin Glasser, M.D.)
   170 Otis Street
   San Francisco, CA 94103

6. *Haldimand Family & Children*
   (Kate Brady)
   653 Broad Street West
   Dunnville, Ontario Canada

7. *Children's Center*
   (Constance Catrone)
   Program Coordinator
   1400 Whitney Avenue
   Hamden, CT 06517

8. *South County Mental Health*
   (Grace Caruso)

16155 South Military Trail
Delray Beach, FL 33445

 9. *Division of Family and Children's Services*
(Linda Doster)
878 Peachtree Street, NE #404
Atlanta, GA 30309

10. *Catholic Charities Department of Social Services*
(V. Bailey)
645 West Randolph Avenue
Chicago, IL 60606

11. *Central Baptist Children*
(Karen Newton)
Program Coordinator
201 N. Wells, Suite 2020
Chicago, IL 60606

12. *Homes for Children*
(Beverly Robie)
1661 North Northwest Highway
Park Ridge, IL 60068

13. *Sullivan House*
(Janice Greer)
Director
7305 South Clyde Avenue
Chicago, IL 60649

14. *Transitional Living Program*
(Patricia Berg)
Director
3179 N. Broadway
Chicago, IL 60657

15. *Methodist Youthville, Inc.*
(Ray Hunsberger)
Director
P.O. Box 210
Newton, KS 67114

16. *The Villages, Inc.*
(Peggy Henry)
P.O. Box 1695
Topeka, KS 66601

17. *Department of Human Resources*
(Carolyn Crosley)
311 West Second Street
Owensboro, KY 42301

18. *Department of Social Services*
(Bruce Scot)
275 E. Main Street, 6W
Frankfurt, KY 40621

19. *Alternate Family Care*
(Richard Caffarel, MSW)
1525 Fairfield Avenue, R. 801
Shreveport, LA 71130

20. *Community Health and Counseling Center*
(Anne Smallidge)
Coordinator
43 Illinois Avenue
Bangor, ME 04401

21. *P.A.T.H.*
(Mike Peterson)
Director
5701 Kentucky Avenue, S. 165
Minneapolis, MN 55428

22. *Area Mental Health*
(Lu Thompson)
Director
125 Emergency Road
Henderson, NC 27536

23. *BIABH Study Center*
(Bob Jones, Ph.D.)
Director, Research
204 Avery Avenue
Morganton, NC 28655

24. *Rowan Co. Department of Social Services*
(Zelma Alston)
1236 West Innes Street
Salisbury, NC 28144

25. *Smoky Mountain Mental Health*
(Roberta Wright)

1207 East Street
Waynesville, NC 28786

26. *Trend Community Mental Health Center*
    (Peggy Goodnough)
    800 North Fleming Street
    Hendersonville, NC 28739

27. *Wake County Department of Social Services*
    (Elaine Rakouskas)
    Superintendent
    P.O. Box 1247
    Raleigh, NC 27602

28. *Youth Care, Inc.*
    (Betty Sherrod)
    1325 Alamana
    Greensboro, NC 27406

29. *Upper Valley Youth Services*
    (Michelle Champoux)
    Coordinator
    On the Mall
    Lebanon, NH 03766

30. *New Mexico Human Services*
    (Archie Edelhart)
    P.O. Box 2348
    Sante Fe, NM 87503

31. *Cummings-Zucker*
    (Mary Beth Henderson)
    Coordinator
    123 22nd Street
    Toledo, OH 43624

32. *Boys and Girls Aid Society*
    (Janet R. Eskridge)
    Coordinator
    2301 N.W. Glisan
    Portland, OR 97210

33. *Casey Family Program*
    (Michael Matern)
    Director
    2705 East Burnside, S. 200
    Portland, OR 97201

34. *Concern, Inc.*
    (Tom Gery)
    1 East Main Street
    Fleetwood, PA 19522

35. *Pressley Ridge School*
    (Pamela Meadowcroft, Ph.D.)
    Director, PRYDE Program
    530 Marshall Avenue
    Pittsburgh, PA 15219

36. *Department for Children and Families*
    (Stephan Lieberman)
    610 Mt. Pleasant Avenue
    Providence, RI 02908

37. *South Carolina Department of Social Services*
    (Jackie H. Davis)
    Box 1520
    Columbia, SC 29202

38. *Juvenile Court Services*
    (Rayna Bomar)
    Coordinator
    Madison County
    Jackson, TN 38301

39. *Northeast Community Mental Health Center*
    (Nita Bogart)
    Coordinator
    5515 Shelby Oaks Drive
    Memphis, TN 38134

40. *Residential Services, Inc.*
    (Charles McLeroy)
    Director
    1007 Murfreesboro Road 115
    Nashville, TN 37217

41. *Community Teaching Homes*
    (Isabel Brintnall, MSW)
    Director
    623 South Pickett Street
    Alexandria, VA 22301

42. *Northern Virginia Special Foster Care*
    (Kathleen Kestner)

Director
100 N. Washington Street #400
Falls Church, VA 22046

43. *People Places, Inc.*
Robert Snodgrass, Ph.D.
Director
1215 North Augusta Street
Staunton, VA 24401

44. *Portsmouth Department of Social Services*
(Jackie Facenda)
700 North Street
Portsmouth, VA 23704

45. *Virginia Baptist Children's Home*
(Carolyn Arthur)
Coordinator
700 E. Belt Boulevard
Richmond, VA 23224

46. *Northeast Kingdom Mental Health Center*
(Carl Bayer)
P.O. Box 214
St. Johnsbury, VT 05819

47. *Lad Lake, Inc.*
(Dennis Neuenfeld)
Director
Box 158
Dousman, WI 53118

48. *Appalachian Mental Health Center*
(Frank Haymond)
Coordinator
P.O. Box 1170
Elkins, WV 26241

II

The Context of
Therapeutic Foster
Care

Introduction to
Part 2

I N PART 2 James Whittaker and Anthony Maluccio caution proponents of therapeutic foster care (TFC) not to let their enthusiasm for their particular mode of treatment lead them to create a straw man by characterizing all group residential care and treatment as one entity, when in fact group care includes several very different kinds of programs. They point out that although the various forms of group residential care and treatment may be more restrictive, some of them may also be more effective. In fact, documented, lasting effectiveness is the real test of the treatment intensity—or potency and breadth—that Robert Hawkins presented in chapter 1. Two other dimensions along which programs might be compared are feasibility and, of course, cost.

Whittaker and Maluccio present some historical highlights of group child care and treatment and the beginnings of some trends within that history. They point out recent developments relative to both group care and TFC, suggesting the implications of these developments for such programs.

One of the most pressing needs in both group and individual residential services is evaluative research. The dearth of evaluations borders on irresponsibility—on the part of not only program developers but also those who pay for the programs—public agencies and insurance companies especially. It is analogous to administering various drugs to millions of relatively defenseless patients—children—without having tested whether the drugs even have beneficial effects, not to mention harmful effects. Whittaker and Maluccio present the results of some studies, briefly, and point out some of the difficulties that have helped to impede outcome evaluations.

Finally, these authors indicate the future developments they see as likely and needed by both group and individual residential services: greater assessment and intervention in the child's ecology; extensive involvement of the child's family (as part of that ecological intervention, but also to maintain the child as part of a family system); and more comprehensive and adequate program evaluation. More was said about the first of these predictions in the Hawkins chapter. More is said later about the second of these, by Maluccio and Whittaker. Robert Friedman addresses the third at the end of the book.

The Carros and Krikston chapter gives an insider's view of the effects within a large public child welfare agency of various, often unpredictable shifts in law, policy, finances, relations with other agencies, and activities of private service-providing agencies. They describe the advantages, limitations, and risks of TFC, a treatment approach with which they are familiar because their agency began one of the longest-standing TFC programs now extant.

They describe their TFC program, which serves both disturbed and retarded youngsters. Although it was not well received by some of the established mental health services, it continues to serve approximately 25 clients. As a collaborative effort between child welfare and the mental health system, it is unique, yet the collaboration seems quite logical in that TFC services comprise both care and treatment.

Changing Paradigms in Residential Services for Disturbed/Disturbing Children: Retrospect and Prospect

JAMES K. WHITTAKER
ANTHONY N. MALUCCIO

T HIS CHAPTER DEALS WITH the history, present health, and future direction of residential care and treatment services for behavior-disordered children.* Its basic premise is that in some important and, probably, as yet unidentified ways, the development and future of therapeutic foster care (TFC) involve many of the same policy and practice issues confronting the field of group child care. Throughout the remainder of the volume, group homes, residential treatment centers, and other forms of youth care are posed as a generic and (generally) less desirable alternative to TFC. This chapter tests the validity of this assumption. It seeks, briefly, to:

> define group child care services
> catalog important milestones in the development of group child care services

*Portions of this review appeared earlier in "Family support and group child care: Rethinking resources" in *Permanence and Family Support: Changing Practice in Group Child Care,* edited by Richard Small and Gary Carmen. Washington, DC: Child Welfare League of America, 1988.

provide a demographic overview of group child care and relate it to present policy

summarize major findings from outcome evaluations

identify trends and issues likely to affect future directions in group child care services

Trends in Residential Services for Children

The Meaning of Group Child Care Services

What do the following services have in common?

A group home for adolescent status offenders

A residential treatment center for emotionally disturbed children

A state training school for adolescent delinquents

A shelter care facility for street children

A respite care group home for developmentally disabled adolescents

A group residence for "dependent/neglected" children

Despite their differences, all of these services fall under the general heading of group child care. This segment of the service continuum is comprised of a number of types of service, each sharing the common element of caring for groups, however small, of special-needs children on a 24-hour-a-day basis. This 24-hour care is the most obvious commonality with TFC. National standard-setting associations recognize several different types of group care settings for children who are dependent and/or have behavioral/emotional difficulties. These include residential treatment centers; group homes; crisis and shelter care facilities; children's psychiatric facilities and respite care facilities [Child Welfare League of America 1984]. Depending upon the state and jurisdictions, group care services for children might be provided under mental health, juvenile correction, child welfare, developmental disabilities auspices, or a combination of two or more of these. Accordingly, there is considerable overlap beween group care services provided by these different authorities, as well as a lack of precision in various definitions of group care. Notice, for example, the similarities in the following definitions offered by the Child Welfare League of America for residential treatment and group home service:

Institutional Care for Children—Residential Treatment (RT)

To provide treatment in a group care therapeutic environment that integrates daily group living, remedial education and treatment services on the basis of an individualized plan for each child, exclusively for children with severe emotional disturbances, whose parents cannot cope with them and who cannot be effectively treated in their own homes, in another family, or in other less intensive treatment-oriented child care facilities. Service elements include: (1) study and diagnosis to determine appropriate service and to develop a treatment plan for each child; (2) work in behalf of or directly with children and youth in a therapeutic milieu during placement (including provision of group living facilities and the essentials of daily living such as dental care, and child care supervision; (3) provision of treatment services as needed by each child (social work, psychiatry, psychology, remedial education); (4) work with parents while child is in placement; (5) postplacement activities during readjustment period.

Group Home Service (GH)

To provide care and treatment in an agency-owned or operated facility that assures continuity of care and opportunity for community experiences, in combination with a planned group living program and specialized services, for small groups of children and youth who are unable to live in their own homes for any reason and who, because of their age, problems, or stage of treatment, can benefit by such a program. Service elements include: (1) assessment to determine the need for and the appropriateness of placement, development of a plan for services, and preparation for placement; (2) if placement is the plan, discharge plans should be included in case planning; (3) work in behalf of or directly with children and youth during placement (including provision of facilities and the essentials of daily living, arrangements for education and recreation; activities congruent with their own religious, cultural, and ethnic traditions; medical-dental care; child car supervision; social work, psychiatry, psychology, vocational and employment guidance and use of other health and welfare services; (4) work with parents while child is in placement; (5) work with parents to strengthen and enhance parental functioning while their children are in placement; (6) post-placement activities during the adjustment period; (7) aftercare services to children, youths, and their families to help them to adjust to the home and community and, when appropriate, to independent living arrangements. [pp. xxiii–xxiv]

Precisely what is meant by such constructs as "therapeutic milieu" is not specified, nor is the implied progression of serving the most "severely disturbed" child in more sophisticated and restricted residential treatment centers empirically borne out in existing programs where severely disturbed children are being treated in less restrictive, more family-oriented settings [Cherry 1976; Dimock 1977; Rubenstein et al. 1978]. Moreover, Maluccio and Marlow's [1972] observation over a decade ago regarding the placement process in institutional care is still largely correct:

> The decision to place a child in residential treatment is presently a highly individualized matter based on a complex set of idiosyncratic factors defying categorization. The literature does not indicate agreement on consistent criteria or universal guidelines and it is not certain whether institutions diverse in origin, philosophy, policy, and clientele can agree on a basic set of premises. [p. 239]

In sum, we must be chary of references to "group and institutional care" as though it were a single entity. It is not. Rather, this segment of the service continuum contains a range of different kinds of residential placements that overlap considerably in terms of definition, purpose, population served, and bureaucratic responsibility. Where a child is placed in this array of group services may depend upon factors external to the child's diagnostic status.

There are, we believe, two relevant comparisons between TFC and the field of group care services. When compared to the field of group care as a whole, including large, custodial institutional settings, TFC will, on almost any indicator of "least restrictiveness" and "normalization," emerge as the desirable service alternative. But another set of comparative questions involves the relative efficacy of TFC as an alternative to residential treatment services, as such. In short, can the kind of treatment programs described in this volume achieve similar or superior results to those of intensive group care services on a range of criterion measures including youth outcomes, consumer evaluations, treatment costs, factors related to normalization, and others.

The most appropriate comparison is with the kind of residential treatment where the living environment is the actual focus for treatment and not simply the place where children live while they receive individualized treatment services. The term therapeutic milieu has been used to describe this process of environmental treatment. Whittaker [1979] defined it as:

> a specifically designed environment in which the events of daily living are used as formats for teaching competence in basic life skills. The living environment becomes both a means and a context for growth and change, informed by a culture that stresses learning through living. [p. 36]

Teaching formats here include things like rule structures, daily routines, play and activities, as well as more individualized education, counseling, and treatment services for children and their parents. Models of residential treatment so defined typically avoid strictly psychogenic explanations of problem behavior and proceed, instead, from an essentially developmental-educational base. This typically involves identification of skill deficits and the teaching of social competence in such areas as managing emotionality, developing more effective interpersonal skills, and mastering proximate and distal community environments. Examples of such residential programs include Project Re-Ed, developed by the late Nicholas Hobbs [1984] in the early 1960s, and the Walker School in Needham, Massachusetts, developed by the late Albert Trieschman [Trieschman et al. 1969; Whittaker 1979].

Obviously, not all residential treatment centers adopt such an integrated approach to the therapeutic milieu. Note, for example, that in the previously cited definition by the Child Welfare League of America treatment services are listed as separate from "work in behalf of or directly with children . . . in a therapeutic milieu." This separation of treatment functions—often along disciplinary lines—has from the beginning been a source of staff conflict and has plagued the development of unified and consistent total milieu approach to working with children [Whittaker and Trieschman 1972; Piliavin 1963; Whittaker 1971b]. Some residential programs, like Project Re-Ed, attempted to overcome this separation of service by combining educational and treatment functions in a single role: the "teacher counselor" [Hobbs 1982]. The Teaching Family model of group home treatment has, similarly, combined all significant helping functions in a single pivotal role, the "teaching parent," with auxiliary support services provided by a training consultant [Phillips et al. 1974]. Ultimately, debate on the relative efficacy of TFC versus other residential treatment programs will improve with the ability to specify the essential dimensions and components of both kinds of services.

Historical Highlights of Group Child Care Services

The "century-old debate" between group care and foster family care detailed by Wolins and Piliavin [1964] continues today. This debate has, from its inception, engendered controversy, criticism, and countercriticism—much of it finding its most articulate and passionate expression in leaders of the institutional and foster care field itself. To wit:

> As a permanent home for the early years of dependent children, the orphan asylum should go out of business. [Reeder 1925: 286]

> The foster home is not a panacea for social ills and should not be advertised as the "Soothing Syrup" of social work. [in reply to Reeder: Langer 1925: 624]

In some ways, the present debate over the relative merits of residential treatment and TFC is a current example of this controversy. For group care and treatment services, some of the more important historical milestones are:

> The establishment of an orphanage by the Ursuline nuns of New Orleans (1729) to care for children orphaned by an Indian massacre at Natchez—the first children's institution in

the present boundaries of the United States [Bremner 1970: 60–61; Whittaker 1971a].

The House of Refuge, first institution for juvenile delinquents founded in New York. Similar institutions founded in Boston (1826) and Philadelphia (1928) [Bremner 1970].

The Lyman School, first state reform school for boys, founded in Westborough, Massachusetts (1847) on the model of the German agricultural reformatory. It is not without irony that Lyman School was also the first state training school to close in the now famous "Massachusetts experiment" in deinstitutionalization in the early 1970s [Bremner 1970: 697–711, and Bremner 1974: 1084–1086; see also Coates et al. 1978].

New York Children's Aid Society sends its first band of children to the west in 1855. What Charles Loring Brace and others saw as saving children from the evil influences of the city and congregate institutions, others—notably, the Irish Catholic community in New York City where children were most affected—saw as a nativist plot to separate their children from their culture, family, and religion. One direct outgrowth of this placing-out movement was the growth of Catholic and other denominational institutions to care for destitute, dependent, and neglected children [Bremner 1970: 669–670; 747–750].

The move in the late 19th century from congregate to cottage-style institutions with an attempt to achieve a more family-like atmosphere [Rothman 1980: 265–283].

The inception and growth of the mental hygiene movement, beginning with the work of Healy in Chicago, with its emphasis on classification of childhood disorders, differential diagnosis and treatment [Bremner 1970: 536–538; Whittaker 1971b].

The slow transition of many children's institutions in the 1930s, 1940s, and 1950s from care of, essentially, dependent children to residential treatment of emotionally disturbed children [Bettelheim and Sylvester 1949; Bremner 1974: 637–643; Mayer and Blum 1971; Redl and Wineman 1957].

Recent exposure of abuse/neglect in residential institutions for disturbed and delinquent children, coupled with and, in part, responsible for efforts to deinstitutionalize service programs in mental health, juvenile correction, child welfare, and mental retardation [Coates et al. 1978; Hanson 1982; National Commission on Children in Need of Parents 1979; Taylor 1981; Wolfensberger 1972; Wooden 1976; Child Abuse and Neglect in Residential Institutions 1978].

These events in the history of group child care appear to cluster in four phases:

1. First was a period of *physical separation* that sought to extricate dependent, delinquent, and "defective" children from indiscriminate mixing in almshouses, workhouses, jails, and the like, and provide a separate set of institutions specifically for their use [Whittaker 1971a].

2. Next was a move from *congregate* to *cottage* care, begun in the late 19th century, which sought to replace cold, barracks-style institutions with smaller, family-style units staffed by houseparents. Although the intent of this movement was clear, the resulting cottage (sometimes containing 25-plus children) was often quite large by today's standards, yet it maintained at least some semblance of a family-like atmosphere.

3. The *psychological phase* begun in the early part of the 20th century sought to transfer the central organizational and treatment concepts of the emergent child guidance movement to the institution [Whittaker 1971b]. These included use of psychological tests, the psychiatric team concept, and the delineation of child care and child treatment functions. Later, the pioneering work of Hershel Alt, Bruno Bettelhiem, Fritz Redl and others in the late 1940s and early 1950s developed various psychoanalytically grounded expressions of the therapeutic milieu with much more attention to factors like group dynamics and a much greater focus on child care staff members as primary agents of treatment.

4. Finally, what might be called the *ecological or environmental phase* was stimulated at least partly by an increasing corpus of outcome evaluations (reviewed briefly later) that showed that differences in treatment outcome were more related to factors like presence or absence of postplacement

community supports than to factors like caseworker judgment, degree of success achieved in program, treatment model, or severity of presenting problems [Whittaker and Pecora 1984]. These findings, as well as the broader policy thrust towards deinstitutionalization and service normalization, forced the attention of residential programs from an almost total preoccupation with what went on inside the milieu to such external factors as development of community linkages, family work, and aftercare. Also contributing to this trend were natural environmental interventions by applied behavior analysts and psychoeducators that boldly moved treatment from the clinic to the client's own milieu [Hawkins et al. 1966; Risley and Wolf 1966; Tharp and Wetzel 1969; Rhodes 1967; Hobbs 1966].

The Demography of Group Child Care and the Present Policy Context

The most systematic and comprehensive census of children in group care was completed by Donnell M. Pappenfort and his colleagues at the University of Chicago, School of Social Service Administration. This survey, for the focal year 1981, updates an earlier survey conducted by Pappenfort in 1965 [Dore et al. 1984; Pappenfort et al. 1973; Pappenfort et al. 1983]. The survey included residential facilities in virtually all streams of care—mental health, juvenile corrections, and child welfare, for example—and identified the following trends:

> While the number of residential group care facilities has increased markedly since 1966, there has been a decline in the number of children in care.
>
> The rate of growth has been concentrated in two areas: facilities for children considered delinquent or status offenders and mental health facilities.
>
> Facilities in all categories have declined in size over the past 16 years. In 1966, less than 50% of the facilities surveyed had fewer than 26 children in residence. Yet the majority of facilities surveyed in 1982 were of that size.
>
> Among the facilities surveyed in 1982, the number of children were almost evenly divided between public and private facilities. Slightly more than one-third of all children were in juvenile justice facilities, one-fourth were in mental

health facilities, and about one-fifth were in child welfare facilities.

In all, there appear to have been approximately 125,000-plus children in group care in 3,914 facilities in 1981, down from 155,000-plus in 2,138 facilities in 1965. The drop in placement figures reflects both a decline in actual children in care and a decline in the rate of group care placement, from 19.9 per 10,000 children in 1965 to 17.3 per 10,000 in 1981 [Pappenfort et al. 1983].

In certain streams of care, nongovernmental services play a major role. For example, in 1983, 92% of the children in group care services for the emotionally disturbed were in voluntary, nonprofit, and proprietary agencies. Proprietary care is apparently on the rise and presently serves 4.5% of all children in group care and 8.5% of all children in nongovernmental group care [Pappenfort et al. 1983]. Some analysts are concerned with what appears to be a shift of youngsters (especially status offenders) from more traditional streams of care (e.g., juvenile justice) to private drug rehabilitation and psychiatric residential settings that are often proprietary [Schwartz et al. 1983]. Similarly, several investigative accounts in recent years have documented abuses in voluntary agencies, especially some religiously oriented group care services, which often avoid not only public funding but also public licensing [Taylor 1981; Wooden 1976]. These later two categories of group care—private psychiatric placements, often funded directly by third-party payments, and private, voluntary placements in religious institutions that avoid both public funding and licensing—constitute what some have called the "hidden sector" of group care.

A central factor underlying present policy for all out-of-home services for children is that in the aggregate, the children represent less than one percent of the nation's 0- to 17-year-olds [Select Committee on Children, Youth, and Families 1983]. This fact may explain, in part, why group care and foster care have not ranked higher on the national policy agenda.* The overwhelming majority of American children live with one or both biological parents or in adoptive homes, as shown in table 1.

The relative lack of visibility for foster care—unlike concern for the developmentally disabled (approximately 10% of the population)—

---

*See Steiner [1981] for additional analysis of why foster care reform has lagged behind other initiatives.

TABLE 1—FAMILY ENVIRONMENT

1. Family Living Arrangements. As of 1982, 14 million young people—or 22% of all children under 18—were living in a single-parent family with either their mother or father. Some 23 million young people—or 37% of all U.S. children under 18—were living in something other than a family where both biological parents were present.

	U.S. Children Under 18—1982	
	Number *(in millions)*	*Percentage of* *All Children*
Child Lives with:		
Both biological parents	39.3	63 %
Mother only	12.5	20
Father only	1.2	2
One biological parent and one stepparent	6.2	10
Grandparents or other relatives	1.6	2
Foster parents, other non-relatives, or in institutions	0.4	1
Total	**62.4**	**100 %**

Source: Calculated from unpublished data from the March, 1982 Current Population Survey data, U.S. Bureau of the Census. Proportions adopted and living with remarried parents estimated from the 1976 and 1981 National Surveys of Children, and from Paul Glick "Children of Divorced Parents in Demographic Perspective," *Journal of Social Issues* 35, 170–182, 1979. (Select Committee 1983)

may be either the cause or consequence of the situation described by Steiner [1981]:

> Foster care has been no First Lady's "principal interest," nor has a secretary of HEW taken it on as a personal crusade. Consequently, it did not receive the high-level attention in the late 1970s that was briefly accorded mental health policy and the dangers of cigarette smoking. Because foster care neither

makes a substantial difference in the federal budget nor involves millions of people, it does not automatically command attention. Scandal does provide occasional visibility, but it is scandal usually limited to childrearing practices, in a particular setting rather than intolerable scandal entailing fraud in benefit claims or other continuing misuse of public money. [p. 144]

Whether foster care will ever become a first lady's interest remains to be seen. Thus it is all the more impressive, given the small percentage of children in care, that foster care reform did surface on the national political agenda, culminating in the passage of Public Law 96–272: The Adoption Assistance and Child Welfare Act of 1980. The intent of this act is to provide permanent homes for children cast adrift in the foster care system, either through return to biological parents or placement for adoption. For those families at risk of disruption, the act mandates that "reasonable efforts" at prevention of placement be carried out and a judicial review be made before placement. Various other provisions have to do with conducting an inventory of all children in the foster care system and providing special subsidies for adoption of special-needs children. The means for achieving these objectives include development of statewide information systems, case review procedures, judicial review of placements, preventive family-oriented services, and development of statewide plans for child welfare services. In general, staged implementation of various reform components is required for continuance of federal funding for foster care payments, although the Reagan administration gave over to the states considerably more latitude in determining compliance than was the case with the original regulations from the Department of Health and Human Services. While it is still too early to assess the overall impact of P.L. 96–272, the U.S. Children's Bureau recently estimated that both the total number of children in foster care and the mean length of stay have declined markedly since the Shyne and Schroeder [1978] national estimate study [U.S. Children's Bureau 1983].* Other findings gleaned from several studies subsequent to the passage of the legislation are as follows:

*More recently, the drugs and AIDS problems, particularly in some urban localities, have given rise to foster care placements through family breakdowns and the birth of afflicted babies.

There are approximately equal numbers of males and females in foster care.

The percentage of the foster care population of minority children appears to be about 40% to 45%.

About 70% of children in foster care live in foster family homes.

Return to parents and relatives is the placement goal for 40% of the children in substitute care, while 49% actually do return home.

Three-fourths of the children entered foster care because of family-related reasons and over three-fourths of these were for abuse and neglect [U.S. Children's Bureau 1983].

The findings presented thus far and the conclusions that are relevant to TFC general policy direction contained in P.L. 96–272 suggest several things. First, the case for placement of any sort will be more difficult to make and will rest on the presumption that reasonable efforts have been made to keep the child and family together. Second, if one assumes that the primary candidates for TFC are those children presently served in group care settings, the potential pool of applicants—at least from the child welfare funding stream—represents less than 30% of the total number of children in a declining population of children in all forms of substitute care. Third, out-of-home placement will increasingly be time-limited and used primarily as a therapeutic tool to help rehabilitate the family, rather than as an end in itself. Finally, that the overwhelming majority of placed children are in care for reasons of abuse and neglect suggests that a strictly child-focused strategy devoid of an aggressive and comprehensive family intervention component will not succeed.

Implications of Outcome Research on Residential Treatment Services

Again, briefly, what does the outcome research tell us about the effectiveness of residential treatment? The short answer is, "it depends." It depends on how one reads the data, when one reads the data, and how confident one is about the methodology of the various investigators. To take the last first, methodological problems involving internal and external validity and reliability abound in evaluations of residential treatment. Typically, these involve absence of control/contrast groups; absence of random assignment; vaguely defined service units; narrow or inappropriate selection of outcome criteria; biased sample selection; and observer/rater bias [Whittaker 1984]. On the remaining question of how and when one reads the data, the following generalizations appear to be borne out across many studies. First, if one limits analysis to objective indicators of adjustment, like school behavior, court contacts and the like, residential treatment fares rather poorly. On more subjective indicators, such as therapists' judgment of progress and various forms of consumer evaluation, residential treatment appears to be rather effective. Second, if one samples behavior during residential treatment, or immediately at discharge from the treatment milieu, residential treatment looks reasonably effective; but if one samples behavior at increasing intervals in such distal environments as school, community, and family, the decay of treatment effects appears to be pronounced.

Bearing in mind the caveats on the potential weaknesses in research design and the difficulties in interpretation of results, the corpus of outcome research in residential treatment yields several general findings. First, the postdischarge environment appears to be a powerful factor in determining successful long-term adjustment, irrespective of gains made while in the program. Studies by Allerhand et al. [1966], Taylor and Alpert [1973], Cavior et al. [1972] and others all support this general finding. The Allerhand et al. study, which involved extensive follow-up of 50 graduates of a sophisticated residential treatment agency (Bellefaire) in Ohio, summarizes the major findings as follows:

> Perhaps the most striking finding of the study is that none of the measurements of within-Bellefaire performance at discharge, either in casework or in cottage and school roles, were useful in themselves in predicting postdischarge adaptability and adaptation. Only when the situation to which the child returned was taken into account were performances at Bellefaire related to postdischarge adequacies. In a stressful community situation, strengths nurtured within the institution tended to break down, whereas in a supportive situation, these strengths tended to be reinforced. [p. 140]

The importance of the postplacement environment was underscored in the later research by Taylor and Alpert, which indicated that contact with biological parents while the child was in placement was positively correlated with postdischarge adjustment. These same researchers conclude that neither the child's presenting symptoms, nor any specific treatment variables were strongly associated with postdischarge adjustment: "[it] is not possible to predict a child's postdischarge adaptation on the basis of a given set of preadmission characteristics" [p. 35]. Similar findings with respect to specific treatment variables and outcome were identified in studies conducted by Davids and his associates. They conclude, "treatment variables, especially conventional psychotherapy, seem to bear little relationship to subsequent adjustment" [Davids et al. 1978].

Part of this lack of demonstrated effect may stem from our still primitive attempts to conceptualize and measure the key treatment variables in a complex intervention like residential treatment. Nelson et al. [1978] found that children who left residential treatment with supportive community ties to family, friends, neighbors, schools, and the like were more likely to maintain their treatment gains than those who did not. Those with support maintained over 70% of their gains, while those without support maintained only 50%. Though the sample size was small (22), this study is notable in that it measured behavior at four points in time beginning with a pretreatment community baseline. Similar results were obtained by Lewis [1982] in a follow-up of a Re-Ed program, though again, small sample size limits generalization.

The similarity of these findings should not be surprising to anyone involved in either service delivery or program evaluation in services to children. The maintenance and generalization of treatment effects, as well as, ultimately, replication of program models remain paramount issues for those involved in mental health services for children. Jones and his colleagues, in their national evaluation of the Teaching Family Model of group home treatment, state the concern as follows:

> TFM (Teaching Family Model) . . . has demonstrated its capability for modifying a wide range of in-program behavior . . . (but) recall that our self-report data suggested little non-maturational change in either deviant or drug behavior across pre-, during, and postprogram phases. The message is simple, a program could be an apparent success if the criterion is modification of target behavior during the program experiences. The same program may be seen as far less successful if the criterion is the postprogram adjustment and reintegration of youth. [Jones et al. 1981: 134]

At this point, while the full meaning of the Jones's findings remains open to question, at the very least they serve to temper the enthusiasm that accompanied earlier evaluations, which reached the conclusion that the Teaching Family Model "works better [than comparison programs] and costs less" (Stumphauzer 1979: 119; Kirigin et al. 1979]. Jones's analysis of national data supports no such conclusion.

Program Needs in Services for Troubled Children and Youth

An Ecological Perspective

As the outcome research so clearly indicates, success in residential care, however defined, is largely a function of the supports available in the posttreatment community environment and has much less to do with either the presenting problem or the type of treatment offered. Consequently, what has come to be known as the "ecological perspective" has profound implications for residential children's services [Whittaker 1978]. It encourages us to view the residential environment as the complex interplay of many different elements both within and outside of the formal service context. Notable here are the quality of the linkages between the residential program and the family, the neighborhood, the peer group, the world of work, and other present and future sources of influence over behavior in the community environment. The Massachusetts experiment in deinstitutionalization, previously mentioned, highlighted the importance of these community linkages as they interact with the formal service program [Coates et al. 1978]. One potential implication of this trend for professionals in residential care is that they will be spending less time in direct treatment of children and more time working with and through the environment, particularly in creating and/or maintaining social support networks for the children and their families [Whittaker 1979; Whittaker and Garbarino 1983]. Specifically, this will mean factoring the environment more prominently into our youth service equation, whether that service occurs in a residential treatment center, TFC home, or the youth's own home. For example, youth care workers will likely:

Teach children *and* families practical skills to cope effectively with their proximate and distal environments.

Work to enhance naturally occurring support networks where they exist, and help to create them where they do not. The carefully conducted research of Wahler and others cautions against overreliance on interpersonal skills training as the sole form of intervention [Dumas and Wahler 1983].

Operate on the premise that "environmental helping" is not synonymous with "aftercare": it begins before placement, continues during placement, and lasts as long after placement as it is needed.

These implications vis-à-vis postplacement support hold for TFC as well. It will be necessary, for example, to learn the extent to which the special foster parents continue to provide important supports to their foster children once the formal service contact has terminated. One might expect more contact/support than in shift-staff settings, but at this point such assertions are unsupported by empirical evidence.

Involvement of Families

If the residential treatment center is to be seen as a temporary support for families in crises, rather than as a substitute for families that have failed, it must engage families as full and equal partners in the helping process. Traditionally, and for a variety of reasons, parents have been kept at arms length from the process of treatment in institutional settings. In the *Challenge of Partnership* [Maluccio and Sinanoglu 1981], the contributors document a variety of ways in which parents of children in foster and residential care can assume a meaningful role in helping. These include parenting skills training; family-support groups; family participation in the life-space of the residential institution; and family therapy [Whittaker 1981]. As in adoption and foster family care, the enormous potential helping power of parents has only barely been touched. Without a strong family intervention component, it is doubtful that any model of out-of-home treatment (including TFC) can improve significantly on the rather meager results emerging from earlier outcome studies with respect to ultimate community reintegration. Again, the question of which setting—group care or TFC—encourages greater parental involvement remains to be tested empirically.

Residential treatment, as an intervention, is best viewed as part of an overall continuum of care, which includes home-based, family-centered programs designed to prevent unnecessary out-of-home placement; services designed to reunify separated children and families; specialized adoption services; family support and education programs; and the kinds of therapeutic foster care programs that provide the basis for this monograph. These services are best viewed as complementary, though the precise relationships among them with respect to such matters as criteria for intake are anything but clear at this time. In all areas of youth services we possess only primitive technologies of change and even more primitive methodologies for measuring their effects.

Comprehensive Evaluation

Perhaps the greatest single lesson to be learned from the recent history of residential treatment is the need to guard against the premature enthusiasm and premature tendency to generalize and overinterpret from incomplete evaluations. Such lessons should not be lost on advocates of therapeutic foster care. Problems like maintenance and generalization and community reintegration will be with us for years to come, and they cannot define the entire set of criterion variables against which programs are measured. As a case in point, the frequently cited Teaching Family model—while somewhat disappointing in its lack of distinctive effects in distal environments—has taught us a great deal about the proximate environment: the treatment setting. This model illustrates how a program can document what its component parts consist of; how those processes can be tracked and evaluated; and how married couples can be effectively trained to carry out program objectives. In fact, it is heartening to note that the TFC programs under discussion have drawn so heavily on portions of the Teaching Family technology, and have used it as a model in other ways, molding it and refashioning it to launch new programs. Their commitment, as with the earlier pioneers in the Teaching Family model, is to rigorous evaluation of both *processes* and *outcomes* [McSweeney et al. 1982]. Evaluation of this kind, whatever it ultimately delivers in successful outcomes, will almost certainly provide us with rich, data-based inferences from which to launch the next generation of experiments, that is, even better programs. For the present, we would do well to avoid viewing therapeutic foster care and group child care as dichotomous services. We intend, instead, to examine more minutely the treatment process variables involved in each, and their relation to desired child and family outcomes.

REFERENCES

Allerhand, M. E.; Weber, R.; and Haug, M. 1966. *Adaptation and adaptability: The Bellefaire follow-up study.* New York: Child Welfare League of America.

Bettelheim, B., and Sylvster, E. 1949. A therapeutic milieu. *American Journal of Orthopsychiatry* 18: 191–206.

Bremner, R. H. 1970, 1974. *Children and youth in America: A documentary history.* Vols. 1 and 3. Cambridge, MA: Harvard University Press.

Cavior, E. C.; Schmidt, A.; and Karacki, L. 1972. *An evaluation of the Kennedy Youth Center Differential Treatment Program.* Washington, DC: U.S. Bureaus of Prisons.

Cherry, T. 1976. The Oregon child study and treatment centers. *Child Care Quarterly* 5: 146–155.

Child abuse and neglect in residential institutions. 1978. NCCAN, DHEW Pub. # (OHDS) 78-30160. Washington, DC: U.S. Government Printing Office.

Child Welfare League of America. 1984. *Directory of member agencies.* New York: Child Welfare League of America.

Coates, R. B.; Miller, A. D.; and Ohlin, L. E. 1978. *Diversity in a youth correctional system.* Cambridge, MA: Ballinger.

Davids, A.; Ryan, R.; and Salvatore, P. 1978. Effectiveness of residential treatment. *American Journal of Orthopsychiatry* 38: 469–475.

Dimock, E. T. 1977. Youth crisis services: Short-term community-based residential treatment. *Child Welfare* 56: 187–196.

Dore, M. M.; Young, T. M.; and Pappenfort, D. M. 1984. Comparison of basic data for national survey of residential group care facilities: 1966–1982. *Child Welfare* 63: 485–495.

Dumas, J. E., and Wahler, R. G. 1983. Predictions of treatment outcome in parent training: Mother insularity and socioeconomic disadvantage. *Behavioral Assessment* 5: 301–313.

Hanson, R., ed. 1982. *Institutional abuse of children and youth.* New York: Haworth Press.

Hawkins, R. P.; Peterson, R. F.; Schweid, E.; and Bijou, S. W. 1966. Behavior therapy in the home: Amelioration of problem parent-child relations with the parent in a therapeutic role. *Journal of Experimental Child Psychology* 4: 99–107.

Hobbs, N. 1966. Helping disturbed children: Psychological and ecological strategies. *American Psychologist* 21: 1105–1151.

———. 1982. *The troubled and troubling child.* San Francisco: Jossey-Bass.

Jones, R. R.; Weinrott, M. R.; and Howard, J. R. 1981. *Impact of the Teaching Family Model on troublesome youth: Findings from the National Evaluation.* Rockville, MD: NIMH (reproduced by National Technical Information Service, U.S. Department of Commerce, Springfield, VA 22191, PB82-224353).

Kane, R. P., and Chambers G. S. 1961. Seven-year follow-up of children hospitalized and discharged from a residential setting. *American Journal of Psychiatry* 117: 1023–1027.

Kirigin, K. A.; Wolf, M. M.; Braukmann, C. J.; Fixsen, D. L.; and Phillips, E. L. 1979. Achievement place: A preliminary outcome evaluation. In *Progress in behavior therapy with delinquents,* edited by J. S. Stumphauzer. 118–155. Springfield, IL: Charles C. Thomas.

Langer, S. 1925. Reply. *Survey* 54: 624.

Lewis, W. W. 1982. Ecological factors in successful residential treatment. *Behavioral Disorders* 7: 149–156.

Maluccio, A. N., and Marlow, W. D. 1972. Residential treatment of emotionally disturbed children: A review of the literature. *Social Service Review* 46: 230–251.

———, and Sinanoglu, P. A., eds. 1981. *The challenge of partnership: Working with parents of children in foster care.* New York: Child Welfare League of America.

Mayer, M. F., and Blum, A., eds. 1971. *Healing through living: A symposium on residential treatment.* Springfield, IL: Charles C. Thomas.

McSweeney, A. J.; Fremouw, W. J.; and Hawkins, R. P., eds. 1982. *Practical program evaluation methods in youth treatment.* Springfield, IL: Charles C. Thomas.

National Commission on Children in Need of Parents: Final report. 1979. New York: NCCINP.

Nelson, R. H.; Singer, M. J.; and Johnsen, L. O. 1978. The application of a residential treatment evaluation model. *Child Care Quarterly* 7: 164–175.

Pappenfort, D. M.; Kilpatrick, D. M.; and Roberts, R. W., eds. 1973. *Child care: Social policy and the institution.* Chicago: Aldine.

———; Young, T. M.; and Marlow, C. R. 1983. *Residential group care: 1981: 1966 and preliminary report of selected findings from the national survey of residential group care facilities.* Chicago: University of Chicago, School of Social Service Administration.

Phillips, E. L.; Phillips, E. A.; Fixsen, D. L.; and Wolf, M. M. 1974. *The teaching family handbook.* Lawrence, KS: Bureau of Child Research, University of Kansas.

Piliavin, I. 1963. Conflict between cottage parents and caseworkers. *Social Service Review* 37: 17–25.

Redl, F., and Wineman, D. 1957. *The aggressive child.* New York: Free Press.

Reeder, R. R. 1925. Our orphaned asylums. *Survey* 54: 283–287.

Rhodes, W. C. 1967. The disturbing child: A problem of ecological management. *Exceptional Children* 33: 449–455.

Risley, J. R., and Wolf, M. M. 1966. Experimental manipulation of autistic behaviors and generalization into the home. In *Control of human behavior,* vol. 1, edited by R. Ulrich, J. Stachnik, and J. Mabry, 193–198. Glenview, IL: Scott, Foresman.

Rothman, D. J. 1980. *Conscience and convenience: The asylum and its alternatives in progressive America.* Boston: Little-Brown.

Rubenstein, S. J. et al. 1978. The parent therapist program: Alternative care for emotionally disturbed children. *American Journal of Orthopsychiatry* 48: 654–662.

Schwartz, I. M.; Jackson-Beelk, M.; and Anderson, R. 1983. Minnesota's "hidden" juvenile control system: Inpatient psychiatric and chemical dependency treatment. *Unpublished Paper.* University of Minnesota, Hubert H. Humphrey Institute of Public Affairs, 21 pp.

Select Committee on Children, Youth, and Families. A report. 1983. Washington DC: U.S. Government Printing Office.

Shyne, A. W., and Schroeder, A. G. (1978). *National study of social services to children and their families.* Washington, DC: National Center for Child Advocacy.

Steiner, G. 1981. *The futility of family policy.* Washington, DC: Brookings.

Stumphauzer, J. S. 1979. Editorial comments. In *Progress in behavior therapy with delinquents,* edited by J. S. Stumphauzer. 118–119. Springfield, IL: Charles C. Thomas.

Taylor, D. A., and Alpert, S. W. 1973. *Continuity and support following residential treatment.* New York: Child Welfare League of America.

Taylor, R. B. 1981. *The kid business.* Boston: Houghton Miflin.

Tharp, R. G., and Wetzel, R. J. 1969. *Behavior modification in the natural environment.* New York: Academic Press.

Trieschman, A. E; Whittaker, J. K.; and Brendtro, L. K. 1969. *The other 23 hours: Child care work in a therapeutic milieu.* New York: Aldine.

U.S. Children's Bureau. 1983. *Child Welfare Research Note #1.* Washington, DC: Department of Health and Human Services.

Whittaker, J. K. 1971a. Colonial child care institutions: Our heritage of care. *Child Welfare* 50: 396–400.

———. 1971b. Mental hygiene influences in children's institutions: Organization and technology for treatment. *Mental Hygiene* 55: 444–450.

———. 1978. The changing character of residential child care: An ecological perspective. *Social Service Review* 22: 21–36.

————. 1979. *Caring for troubled children: Residential treatment in a community context.* San Francisco: Jossey-Bass.

————. 1981. Family involvement in residential child care: A support system for biological parents. In *The challenge of partnership: Working with parents in foster care,* edited by A. N. Maluccio and P. Sinanoglu, 67–89. New York: Child Welfare League of America.

————. 1984. Formal and informal helping in child welfare services: Implications for management and practice. *Child Welfare* 65: 17–25.

————; Garbarino, J.; and associates. 1983. *Social support networks: Informal helping in the human services.* New York: Aldine.

————, and Pecora, P. 1984. *A research agenda for residential care.* In *Group care practice: The challenge of the next decade,* edited by J. Philpot, 71–87. Surrey, United Kingdom: Community Care/ Business Press International.

————, and Trieschman, A. E., eds. 1972. *Children away from home: A sourcebook of residential treatment.* New York: Aldine.

Wolfensberger, W. 1972. *Normalization.* New York: National Institute on Mental Retardation.

Wolins, M., and Piliavin, I. 1964. *Institution and foster family: A century of debate.* New York: Child Welfare League of America.

Wooden, K. 1976. *Weeping in the playtime of others.* New York: McGraw-Hill.

A Public Child Welfare Agency Perspective on Therapeutic Foster Care

THOMAS N. CARROS
DANIEL KRIKSTON

T HE AUTHORS, RESPECTIVELY, direct a large, public child welfare agency and a long-established therapeutic foster care (TFC) program within that agency, the Allegheny County Children and Youth Services, Pittsburgh, Pennsylvania.* Thus, we represent both the perspective of a public agency that pays for TFC—along with many other child services—and the perspective of an experienced therapeutic foster care service.

This chapter first decribes the statutory, regulatory, and financial context of the agency; continues with an overview, including the numbers of children who receive various services, trends observed over the past several years, and the role that TFC plays in meeting children's needs; and concludes with a description of the agency's TFC program and impressions gained from over 15 years of experience with it.

*Positions held until 5/85 and 3/86, respectively.

The Statutory, Regulatory, and Fiscal Context

The public child welfare program in Pennsylvania is a county-administered, state-supervised system. The legal mandates passed by the state legislature give to the 67 counties in Pennsylvania the responsibility of providing services to dependent and neglected children and families in and/or out of their homes, and establish the base for the state's fiscal participation.

State laws concerned with child abuse place upon the county child welfare agency the responsibility of responding to child abuse referrals, providing service, keeping records, and so forth. The dispositional powers granted to Juvenile Court are contained in other legislation and provide the court the option, among others, of giving custody of children to the public child welfare agency. The agency also can be granted guardianship by the Orphan's Court, with the right to consent to adoption.

The State Department of Welfare, Office of Children, Youth, and Families promulgates regulations to implement the legislation passed by the legislature and/or necessary to receive federal funds. Regulations determine the types of services given, reimbursement, personnel practices, fiscal and other procedures, standards, and service expectations.

As a result, what has developed in the Commonwealth of Pennsylvania is a child welfare program with a uniform definition of basic program requirements that all counties are expected to meet if they are to obtain state certification/approval and state and federal funds. At the same time there is local county administration of programs.

The county administration of the program allows some administrative latitude, including the making of decisions regarding purchase of services. The law requires that programs meet state licensing requirements for the county to be eligible for reimbursement, but counties are able to decide, from the programs available, those they wish to use.

Role of Children and Youth Services

Allegheny County Children and Youth Services (CYS) provides child welfare services in Allegheny County, which includes the City of Pittsburgh and has a population of approximately 1,500,000 persons. Of this total, 22% or approximately 316,000, are persons in the 0 to 17 age range. The services provided are intake, referrals to other agencies, child protective services, emergency care, homemaker services, and adoption (including subsidized adoptions).

The agency provides direct care through operation of a regular foster home care program, emergency care, a TFC program, intake, protective services, adoption, and homemaker services. Services are also purchased from private organizations for in- and out-of-home programs. The great majority of private providers of services are not-for-profit (voluntary) agencies. A few for-profit (proprietary) agencies also exist and are used for services. This chapter uses the term "private" to include both kinds of agencies.

As of March 31, 1984, the regular foster home care program was serving 797 children directly and in foster home care purchased from private providers. In addition, approximately 300 children were placed in other child caring facilities: institutions, group homes, independent-living arrangements, and day treatment. As of the same date, 247 children were in adoptive homes with 208 receiving adoption subsidies. The total number of children in all out-of-home placement was 1,461.

The CYS staff numbers 350 persons, comprising administrative, casework, fiscal, personnel, training, child care, homemaker, caseaide, clerical, nursing, custodial, and maintenance personnel. The total budget was $22,330,000. The total number of children receiving services on March 31, 1984, was 8,423, of which 6,962 children (82.64%) were living with their parents or relatives. CYS has necessarily played a central role as the developer/facilitator of resources for children.

Role in Developing and Facilitating Services for Children

The original, informal division of labor between CYS, when it was started in 1963, and the private agencies in the area was based on the idea that the public agency would provide foster care to children "without serious problems." The agency would depend upon the private agencies for services to children with "serious" problems, or those who needed special care. This arrangement was workable, in the main, for several years, until 1971. At that time it became increasingly evident that the types of cases being referred to CYS for placement were children who had been in special programs and/or other facilities and had not been successfully served in those programs. As a result, many children were in the CYS emergency shelter, or awaiting placement with no place to go. It became obvious, also, that CYS was holding a growing number of children with multiple diagnoses: dependent, mentally ill, and/or mentally retarded. CYS appeared to have two options. One, which was undertaken, was a renewal of efforts to encourage the development of additional treatment facilities. In the mid-to-late 1970s, CYS facilitated the addition of several group homes and the revamping of other programs, by other organizations, for the purpose of accepting children with the types of behaviors that seemed to make continued placement difficult. The other option was for CYS to develop a TFC program; the decision to do this was made in 1971, and the program is described later.

Throughout the 20 years of CYS's existence, the agency has been concerned not only with increasing foster care resources but with the development of a range of other resources to provide adequately for the children in its care. This included services to children and their families so that the children could stay with their parents, as well as return home from out-of-home placement with a minimum of disruption. Advances have been made in this regard but not to the extent envisioned.

An important reason for the difficulty in providing a full and comprehensive range of placement services is the realization that some children, for a variety of reasons, cannot be with their parents but do not appear to be able to stay with any of the existing out-of-home programs for any length of time. This lack has been a central theme in discussions with private service providers in a variety of meetings and committees over the years. Ways have been devised to minimize the problem, but the agency is still left with a core group of children who do not "fit" into the existing services.

Other developments and important trends from 1970 to the present have influenced the relationship with private providers and the capacity of CYS to provide needed services:

> State legislation amending the Juvenile Act
> State legislation that determines reimbursement, with an emphasis on community-based services and deinstitutionalization
> State reduction in child welfare funds (1980–1981)
> Federal legislation: Public Law 96–272

Inadequate implementation of state mental health and mental retardation programs

State child abuse legislation

All of these developments have involved legislation, both state and federal, which was intended to correct perceived weaknesses or inadequacies in the foster care delivery system and in institution-based services. The main points have been a greater emphasis on protecting the rights of children; development of community-based programs and services to keep families together; and return of children to parents, or other permanent arrangements, in a more expeditious and planned way.

The incentive for the local implementation of these concepts has been receipt of state and federal funds. It is ironic, but not unique, that even with the almost universal acceptance of the values involved in such legislation, the availability of the financial means to accomplish these ends has not been consistent with the demands for service. The end result is a system with expanded horizons and goals, but with fiscal limitations and restrictions. These seemingly contradictory currents have played an important part in the development and greater use of TFC programs.

The Influence of Placement Trends on Services

Several other trends are relevant to TFC. First, for CYS the caseload size, including the number of children in out-of-home placement, increased until 1979 and then declined. This recent decline accords with national statistics, which show a decrease in the number of children in foster care for the same period [Gershenson 1984]. Yet, since January of 1984 the trend has reversed again in Pennsylvania, with foster care placements now increasing [Carros 1984]. The number of children with serious behavioral problems has also increased. A number of reasons help to explain this trend (at least in Pennsylvania), including the failure of the mental health system to provide treatment to mentally ill children [Knitzer 1982], the lack of adequate preventive services, and the greater reporting of child abuse, especially sexual abuse.

This general picture has brought about the use by CYS of private provider facilities in greater proportion than had been true in the past several years. The development of services for difficult youths by private providers has made it possible for the child welfare system to accommodate problems while still using its regular foster care program to respond to the currently increasing demand for foster care.

Purchased TFC

At this writing, TFC is purchased by CYS from eight programs in the county. These programs have been in operation from three to 15 years. The types of children accepted range from slightly disturbed to extremely disturbed, aggressive, and retarded.

Of the 1,461 Allegheny County children in out-of-home placement, 118 are in shelter care, 214 are in institutions, 85 are in group homes, 247 are in adoptive homes, and 797 are in some type of foster home. Of the latter, 151 (19%) are placed with private TFC programs. About 100 (66%) of these 151 are children with serious problems.

To a public agency such as CYS, given the circumstances already outlined, the development and availability of TFC programs provides an alternative and often-needed service—a positive development. CYS recognizes the need to have available programs that provide intensive treatment, in a variety of settings, along with other placement services.

Potential and Realized Advantages of TFC

Advantages identified by proponents of TFC programs [Bryant 1980; Hawkins and Luster 1982] include:

TFC offers good substitutes for institutional programs.

TFC avoids many institution costs, such as the large capital outlay, and building and maintenance costs. Funds can be redirected to staff and treatment.

TFC programs are much more flexible than traditional programs: for example, they can adjust to trends; they do not have to be concerned with unfilled beds and offices; services can be obtained through contractual arrangements and can be easily expanded or changed based on local needs and conditions.

Everyday observations can be made of the child's behavior in natural situations, and these observations can provide the basis for an intervention in the natural environment, in the reality of living together.

TFC programs provide greater opportunities for individual assessment and treatment and important incidental learning. Treatment intensity can be increased, as needed, while restrictive elements are reduced, such as limitations on contact with well-adjusted children, on opportunities to participate in typical recreation activities, on requirements to carry out the normal housekeeping chores of any family, and so on.

TFC does not have the limitations that residential programs have regarding ranges, types, and number of children who can be served at any given point in time.

TFC programs meet the demands of current trends regarding normalization/integration, mainstreaming, deinstitutionalization, and the requirements of P.L. 96–272.

TFC programs offer the possibility of a permanent home if the child has no place to which he or she can return.

TFC programs cost less.

The experience of CYS to date with TFC programs supports the validity of these observed advantages, although more time may be needed to evaluate how each of them is realized in any specific program, especially the newer ones. In general, CYS's experience has been positive with those programs it has used, and CYS has supported the development of such programs, including its own.

Potential and Realized Risks and Limitations of TFC

Some limitations identified by TFC providers have been observed also by CYS staff. One group of limitations has to do with the types of children who might be considered for such programs. Some programs will not admit children with I.Q.s below 65. Some exclude children with significant behavior problems or who are a serious risk to themselves or others. Among those who do admit incorrigible children and youths, some exclude the older ones.

Some programs have difficulty recruiting and selecting foster parents or treatment parents; others experience rather chronic funding problems. Many programs do little or no work with biological parents; and many seem to have difficulty making effective matches between the foster/treatment parents and the children they serve. Of special concern are the demands placed by TFC on both staff members and foster/ treatment parents, including training requirements, travel, and 24-hour exposure to children with severe problems, sometimes leading to burn- out.

In CYS's experience with private agencies conducting TFC pro- grams, several other problems have been noted that relate to CYS's particular role and concerns: minimum consultation with CYS regard- ing discharge planning of children, especially when children are to be returned to their homes; differences between CYS standards for foster home approval and standards used by private providers; lack of depth in the studies of applicant homes; and delays in obtaining a school placement for a youngster.

Some of these problems arise because of inadequate discussion between the agencies and CYS when purchase arrangements are being made; lack of clarity about the roles of respective staff members; differences in philosophy about working with biological parents, es- pecially in relation to legal custody of children and parental respon- sibility; unrealistic expectations by the private agency; or lack of understanding about developing and administering programs. Many of the problems can and have been resolved by timely identification of the problem, CYS's providing a clear policy statement or more information about legal requirements, and arranging for staff members to review program issues in regularly scheduled meetings.

Of specific concern to CYS is how to avoid the "purchase-of-care horror show" that occurs when monitoring/review activities are not mutually defined and adequately implemented. Sometimes the private provider fails to comply with CYS and/or Department of Public Wel- fare regulations. But regulations are not a sufficient criterion, so pro- cedures not covered by regulations need to be identified and agreed upon as a basis for a continuing positive purchaser/provider rela- tionship. Without this, children are easily lost, or crises develop regard- ing particular placements. CYS has found that by assigning one or two staff members to monitor all cases being served by a particular program, communication problems and other difficulties can be minimized.

Another concern is that the state Department of Public Welfare licenses private foster care programs—including TFC—in a manner that precludes the state's evaluation of individual foster homes. As a result, the county agency purchasing the service, such as CYS, has no way of knowing the adequacy of criteria or procedures for approval and retention of foster parents. One possible solution to this problem would be the selection by the Department of Public Welfare of a sample of foster homes, making in-person visits, and evaluating the actual situation with clearly stated standards and criteria. Additional, more informal or partial spot checks by Public Welfare or CYS staff members could supplement these thorough evaluations.

In summary, CYS agrees with the proposition that TFC programs have certain advantages over traditional institutional placement and traditional foster home care. They provide a reasonable alternative for children with special problems who need to be placed out of their own homes. Support of such programs does not imply criticism of the traditional programs, which can and do play an important part in a continuum of services for children at different times in their development. Nor does CYS subscribe to the Pennsylvania policy that provides less reimbursement to county child welfare agencies for congregate, larger facilities because of their size, with the rationale that "community-based" care is more desirable than "institutional" care. A more discriminating approach might be that of evaluating, and including in definitions, program elements that constitute various categories and degrees of treatment and other services. It is not necessarily true that programs are good because of their size or where they are located.

More General Issues Involving Private Service Providers

In examining the relationship between the public agency and private providers, as it pertains not only to TFC but also to other programs, other concerns can be identified. These have been the subject of discussion for a long time and have yet to be satisfactorily resolved. The following are persistent or difficult problems:

> How are program reimbursement rates to be determined?

> How are programs to be monitored/evaluated?

> What should be the content of contracts between public agency and private provider?

> Should competitive bidding be used for all purchase-of-care contracts?

> What is the most efficient and practical way to make referrals of children to providers?

This is not the place to attempt full exposition or resolution of these issues, but it is important for those who consider developing or disseminating TFC programs to be aware that these issues are likely to face them in every community.

Another matter that has been mentioned from time to time but has seen little in the way of actual implementation is that of joint efforts by private and public agencies. For example, joint efforts in recruitment of foster parents, training of foster parents, training of staff members, development of evaluation procedures, and development of other resources (e.g., educational, vocational, counseling, or special treatment) could be very productive. Certainly, the benefits to children and families could be such as to justify the effort. The realization of this goal has usually been elusive, even though it has been often discussed. CYS's joint effort with the County Mental Health/Mental Retardation program appears to be an exception, as discussed below, in the context of describing CYS's own TFC program.

CYS's Specialized Foster Home Program

Program Organization and Funding

The Specialized Foster Home Program (SFHP) is operated by CYS but funded by both CYS and Allegheny County Mental Health/ Mental Retardation Program (MH/MR). The mental health component began in late 1971, and the mental retardation component began in June 1976. The SFHP is a separate unit within the CYS Foster Home Department and depends on the larger CYS agency for fiscal accounting, certain foster home recruitment and study services, stenographic services, case aide services, administrative supervision, and general staff training.

CYS funds one caseworker position and the supervisor position. CYS also provides a basic board payment to foster parents as well as clothing and all other incidental payments that would ordinarily be provided to a CYS foster home. The board payment, which is intended to meet only the child's basic food and shelter requirements, in 1987 ranged from $9.40 to $10.95 per day, depending on the age of the child.

MH/MR funds support the project director position and one caseworker position. MH/MR funds pay for a "board supplement" (as in "room and board") to foster parents as well as treatment and supportive supplies, respite care, and miscellaneous evaluation and treatment costs related to the child's disability. The MH/MR board supplement is essentially a fee for services in recognition of the additional work required of foster parents in helping to carry out the child's treatment program. The 1987 range in the amount of the supplement was $10.00 to $19.00 per day; the average rate for disturbed youngsters was $11.30; the average daily rate for retarded youngsters was $13.73.

Some children contribute to the cost of their care, using Supplemental Security Income (SSI) benefits. These benefits are assigned to specific CYS and MH/MR costs according to a prescribed disbursement formula.

Client Population and Program Goals

The SFHP is a treatment program that provides 24-hour foster home care and treatment services using agency and community resources. It is intended to be not only a community-based alternative to institutional care for youngsters who qualify, but also a postinstitutional and posthospital placement. Other candidates for the program include youngsters who are already in foster care or are to be placed in foster care and who, without specialized and more intensive services, are at high risk for failure because of their mental retardation or mental health disability. Priority is given to those children whose treatment needs are particularly suited to SFHP treatment resources and who cannot receive suitable service by using outpatient MH/MR resources alone.

The child poulation may range in age from several months to 21 years. The child must be either mentally retarded (I.Q. under 70) or emotionally disturbed (mental health disability), as determined by psychological and psychiatric evaluations. Medical disabilities may also accompany this basic disability. Current program capacity is 10 emotionally disturbed children and 18 mentally retarded children. Youngsters who are not eligible include those who are actively psychotic, adjudicated delinquents, chronic runaways, those who demonstrate chronic and flagrant sexual misconduct, those showing other behaviors that pose a serious threat to the safety of the child or community, and youngsters who can be managed in their own homes.

Length of involvement in the SFHP may range from six months to years, depending upon the child's disability and response to treatment.

Retarded children tend to be in placement longer than emotionally disturbed children, who are more likely to move into the regular foster home program unless they are able to return to the care of their parents. A move from SFHP to regular foster care usually involves the child remaining in the same home but receiving a reduction in the intensity of services and transfer of responsibility for the child from a SFHP caseworker to a regular foster care caseworker. The MH/MR funded board rate supplement is also terminated. A specific effort is also made to raise the self-care and social skills level of the retarded child to a degree that return home or adoption is a viable alternative. Short-term, follow-up service to children who are returned home is also provided by SFHP staff and behavior management specialists to supplement services available from other community treatment and social service resources.

Collaborative Relationship Between CYS and MH/MR

Referral.   Collaboration begins at the point of the child's referral through the local MH/MR Base Service Unit. The Base Service Unit (BSU) is a local MH/MR service and administrative entity responsible for the needs of MH/MR clients who reside in a specific catchment area. In addition to providing certain outpatient and education services, BSUs also determine eligiblity for, and authorize admission to, a variety of MH/MR-funded treatment, rehabilitative, and residential services throughout the county, including the CYS SFHP.

All referrals to the SFHP, whether they originate from within CYS or from an outside agency, must come through the MH/MR BSU in which the parents of the referred child live. If the BSU confirms the existence of a mental health or mental retardation disability and if it concurs with the referral request, a copy of the referral material and any additional assessment material is forwarded to the SFHP dirctor. The SFHP director notifies the BSU as to the acceptance of the referred child and the availability of an appropriate foster home.

Treatment planning.   After acceptance of a referral by the SFHP director, an individualized treatment plan for the accepted client is formulated and the child and foster family are prepared for placement. The treatment plan provides identifying information, reason for referral to the SFHP, description of the child's routine and special needs, resources and strategies to meet the specified needs, the extent of and arrangements for biological family involvement, and pertinent legal information, including the court order from the county juvenile court giving permission for placement outside the child's own home. The treatment plan is intended to be a synopsis of all the pertinent elements of the child's care/treatment plan, including caretakers, responsible CYS and MH/MR staff persons, and medical and other treatment providers. It is a reference and accountability tool and is not intended to be a substitute for the CYS case record or the detailed behavior management treatment records.

Admission. After the treatment plan is completed by the SFHP staff, it is reviewed and confirmed by the appropriate BSU representative, the SFHP director and/or supervisor, and a SFHP caseworker, and the child is formally admitted into the SFHP. The amount of MH/MR board supplement to be paid to the foster parents is also determined at this meeting. This supplement is figured on a sliding scale basis, using a form intended to reflect the extent of care the child will need and the degree of foster parent involvement beyond that required of a normal child. Each board supplement is reviewed at least annually and adjusted to reflect the child's current needs and the corresponding degree of foster parent involvement.

Collaboration during placement. The SFHP informs the appropriate BSU of the child's progress by submitting a copy of the semiannual treatment plan. This plan for each child is reviewed at a joint semiannual conference by BSU staff, CYS staff, and the MH/MR supervisor of admissions and discharge. The BSU may also elect to have its representative visit the child in the foster home for one on-site visit per year. In those instances where the BSU is providing some direct service to the child, the flow of information will be substantially greater than that supplied by the semiannual treatment plan.

Staff and Service of the Specialized Foster Home Program

CYS staff. The program director is responsible for evaluation of referrals, overall program supervision, planning, program development, and administration related to contracts and fiscal reports. Assisting the program director is one supervisor. The supervisor monitors and directs the two caseworkers' activity and assists the director in evaluation of referrals, resource utilization, and program development.

Both caseworkers hold M.S.W. degrees and are responsible for the development, implementation, and monitoring of individual treatment plans, including coordination of all in-agency and out-of-agency resources used by the child. The caseworker maintains a current record of each child's history, medical care, progress, and the activities of CYS and others in behalf of the child. In addition, the caseworker provides direct supportive services to the foster parents to enhance their responsiveness to the child's needs and implementation of their portion of the treatment plan.

The caseworker also gives special attention to the biological family in the treatment process. The caseworker must assess the role of the biological family in this process and plan for the type and frequency of contact between the biological family and the child in foster care. Planning for biological family involvement is viewed not only in the context of treatment goals, but also in the larger context of the CYS mission to protect children and work for the stabilization and unification of families. This element distinguishes the treatment focus of the CYS Specialized Foster Home Program from other clinical approaches that focus predominantly on symptom reduction or behavioral change apart from family systems issues and reunification of the child in care with the biological family.

The frequency and nature of caseworker involvement with the biological family varies according to the needs and circumstances of each child. Involvement may range from limited in cases where parents have essentially abandoned the child to intense involvement in cases where return of the child to the family is the plan, necessitating parent-child conflict resolution, parenting skills training, and generalization of treatment strategies from the foster home environment to the biological family environment. The caseworker might provide all individual and family services directly or work in conjunction with other agency staff members or community resources in providing the necessary services.

Although the SFHP caseworker is usually responsible for services to both the child in placement and the biological family, in those cases requiring more extensive and longer-term protective services for siblings residing in the biological family home, a CYS general family services caseworker will be assigned to serve the biological family. This shared service arrangement allows the SFHP caseworker to give the necessary time and attention to the treatment needs of the child in care.

Foster parents.   The foster parents are responsible for day-to-day care of the child and for implementing portions of the physical therapy and behavior management programs.

Given the small and gradual increase in admissions to the SFHP each year, there is no widespread recruitment program. Foster parents tend to be either already active as CYS foster parents or identified in the course of the Recruitment and Placement Resources Department's initial home evaluation as having the potential for serving children with disabilities. Some foster parents are referred from outside the agency along with the referred child because of a previous interest in the child.

All foster parents who are new to CYS must complete a mandatory 12-hour (six weekly, two-hour sessions) orientation course, plus a minimum of six hours of training each year thereafter. The orientation includes the following topics: the role and functions of foster parents; laws, regulations, and policies related to foster care, with special mention of the regulation that forbids the use of corporal punishment; realistic expectations and special needs of foster children; biological parents and their legal and psychological impact in the life and placement of the child; basic parenting skills; and the placement process. During orientation, foster parent candidates also have an opportunity to talk with experienced CYS foster parents.

All foster parents in the SFHP are further prepared, individually, to manage the child in their care. This is done by their caseworker and by the behavior management specialist consultant to the program, whose role is described later. Foster parents taking children with medical disabilities are provided with additional instruction by the medical facility or practitioner who is active with that youngster. Moreover, foster parents in the SFHP meet voluntarily on a quarterly basis for presentations on subjects related to their work, program and CYS updates, and general information sharing and support.

Nonagency resources and responsibilities. Behavior management services are purchased by CYS on a contractual basis at an hourly fee. At present two child care-behavior management specialists provide services to the child and the child's foster parents in the foster home. Besides regular, planned services to designated children, they provide 24-hour, on-call service to the child and foster parents. Moreover, they also offer consultation and evaluation of the child. Although the CYS caseworkers are responsible for foster parent evaluations, the behavior management specialists contribute to the evaluative process based on their work with specific foster parents.

The SFHP has arrangements with individual psychological and psychiatric professionals for psychological and psychiatric evaluations, case consultation, and education consultation. This allows service to be obtained promptly, with continuity, and only as needed, yet by providers who are familiar with both the individual children served and the overall program.

    Treatment approach and its development.   Given the relative lack of models, the SFHP began as an enhanced version of regular foster home care, and only gradually reached the structure described above. The resources of the agency's regular Foster Home Department were enhanced by using master's degree social workers in all full-time and part-time program positions, by greater utilization of psychiatric and psychological evaluations and consultations, and by training for the program's two staff persons in clinical work with children and families, and in basic behavior modification procedures and theory. In other words, CYS attempted to graft onto traditional foster care those treatment modalities that were found in the typical child guidance clinic or mental health facility.

    While SFHP had many "successes"—children whose functioning improved and who had stable placements—during the first five years of operations, there was also an approximate 25% failure rate. The failures tended to cluster in the 11- to 14-year-old age range. These youngsters showed persistently poor response to direction, excessive need for adult supervision and intervention, poor retention and generalization of learned appropriate behaviors, lying and stealing, aggressiveness, poor self-image, low motivation, and a strong need for physical gratification. In comparison with residential treatment facilities, SFHP was failing at roughly the same rate with a similar but slightly younger population.

    With increased experience, the weaknesses both within the program and in the resources within the larger community became more evident. In regard to the program, it was difficult to predict, with sufficient accuracy and regularity, which foster parents would be effective in working with the SFHP youngsters. Moreover, while clinical skills generated greater insight into client problems, family dynamics, and reasons for placement failure, these skills alone did not appear to be sufficient to reach successfully that difficult segment in the program population that comprised the bulk of failed placements. It also became clear that case management responsibilities often competed with direct service objectives. Intensive counseling and teaching of skills by the casework staff could not be sustained for prolonged periods. Established community resources—hospitals, clinics, child development centers, and mental health centers—responded variably both toward the SFHP itself and to the needs of the youngsters. Some were very responsive, flexible, and interested in the SFHP approach. Others could not accept the program as a legitimate treatment modality; at times it appeared that they judged professional legitimacy not by treatment outcome but by the treatment setting, staff credentials, and proper usage of psychiatric jargon. That the SFHP was a public agency program only served to further seal the staff's status as paraprofessionals.

In 1976, when the program was expanded to serve mentally retarded youngsters, it was thought that the most difficult clients would be the severely retarded, medically handicapped youngsters, but it was the moderately retarded child with persistent behavioral problems who presented the greatest treatment challenge. In other words, the behaviors that led to failed placements for retarded youngsters were the same ones that led to the failure of placements of emotionally disturbed youngsters; the level of retardation was not the critical variable.

A positive step toward meeting this challenge occurred when a woman with previous child care experience in group home settings and with considerable behavior management skill became a foster parent for a retarded, seriously disturbed teenager. Her success led CYS to contract for additional services from her and another behavior management specialist for problematic youngsters in other specialized foster homes. Services included staff consultation, individualized foster parent training, directed behaviorally oriented treatment to foster children in their respective foster homes, and 24-hour, on-call crisis intervention services. The addition of this in-home behavior management component to the treatment team brought about more intense, consistent, and individualized treatment for the children, stronger support for the foster parents, accelerated progress by the children, and reduced placement failure in both the emotionally disturbed and mentally retarded segments of the SFHP. Approximately half of the total child population receives supplemental treatment services from the behavior management specialists.

Since 1976, the SFHP has added other new services, further reduced placement failures, and initiated a joint research project with the University of Pittsburgh Psychology Department, which should lead to more compatible and reliable placements. Equally important, the staff has moved toward a better understanding of the program as a distinct treatment model with certain advantages and limitations. The theoretical, attitudinal, and programmatic elements that have emerged as significant include:

Treatment intensity and restrictiveness (as previously defined) of the physical setting are not necessarily correlated;

TFC can be quite intense and individualized, though not very restrictive, as Hawkins and Luster [1982] have indicated.

TFC can be successful with a surprising range of children and problems [Hawkins and Luster 1982].

The focus of treatment must be the whole and dynamic child, his or her relationships with own family and significant others, and the need for the child to become a viable and responsible adult in the community [Meadowcroft et al. 1982]. Treatment as a focus on a static, detached child with isolated symptoms is too limited.

The validity and legitimacy of treatment should be measured by outcome, by benefits to children and their families, not by the stature, credentials, and affiliations of the treatment practitioner.

Program staff members, foster parents, and consultants must be compatible in regard to program goals, philosophy, and the elements of treatment practice.

A strong behavior management component should exist in the program, although not necessarily used in a formal way with every child and family.

Capable foster parents are critical to program success and must be viewed as treatment team members.

Program staff members at all levels must be mutually supportive and share a determined "whatever it takes" attitude [Hawkins and Luster 1982]; determination is critical not only in working with children and their families but also in dealing with the larger community resource network, which can be fragmented, unresponsive, and even oppositional. Accountability, self-assessment, and openness to change are especially important in TFC, because the structure and operation are less defined by tradition, physical setting, and accepted role definitions [Hawkins and Meadowcroft 1984; Hawkins et al. 1985].

Child and family problems, needs, strengths, and treatment activity must be stated in terms that are specific and understandable to all members of the treatment team and should be derived from observable data and reliable measures.

Value of SFHP in the Agency, and Other Considerations

Although Allegheny County CYS is a large agency with a substantial need for placement resources, the SFHP has remained relatively small. The size of the program has been restricted by the amount of MH/MR funding available, limited foster home resources, and CYS program goals. The intent of the program has been to supplement, not substitute for, a range of placement options for children, including other family-based placement services purchased by CYS.

The SFHP in its present form and size has been a satisfying undertaking in a variety of ways beyond serving the needs of children and families. It has afforded program staff members the opportunity and resources to develop and practice skills ordinarily beyond the scope of public agency practice. The experience and expertise generated, it is hoped, will generalize to other areas of agency practice and training. It has already provided CYS with its own benchmark to measure the performance of private placement providers. Moreover, the SFHP has provided a valuable link with the MH/MR system both in terms of a vehicle by which MH/MR can participate in the cost of serving dependent children with disabilities and also as a practical forum for joint planning in larger interagency policy and service issues.

In several areas, the SFHP continues to experience gaps or deficiencies in program integrity and in meeting the demand for services to new clients. The small number of staff members and the longevity of employment of key staff members have allowed for a continuity of goals and service standards through an oral tradition with limited written policies, procedures, and measurement tools. This deficiency needs to be corrected to ensure future program stability and quality, especially if program expansion or major staff changes take place.

The dependence of the program on the larger CYS agency for foster home recruitment and hiring of new staff members through a cumbersome civil service mechanism, as well as fixed MH/MR funding, has generated periodic problems in maintaining program efficiency. It is difficult to coordinate the elements of funding, staff, and resources while having only limited control of these variables. Programs in the private sector appear to be better able to maintain more efficient ongoing staff and foster home recruitment efforts to meet new service demands in a more timely manner.

At present, CYS is undergoing substantial changes, including moving from specialty caseloads and services to generic caseloads. The SFHP is expected to continue, however. As part of an agency-wide effort to reduce child placement costs, expansion of the SFHP with additional CYS funds and pursuing a more aggressive foster parent recruitment effort are being studied. Expansion could be economically beneficial. Because the SFHP is incorporated within the larger CYS agency, operating costs are spread over a larger base. Given reduced operating costs and MH/MR funding, CYS can deliver specialized foster care at a lower cost than is usually found in the private sector. With increased agency service capacity, CYS could continue to purchase placement services from the most cost- and service-efficient TFC programs while reducing or eliminating purchased placement services from those residential facilities or TFC programs in the private sector that are less cost- and treatment-effective and less responsive to CYS client service needs and agency objectives.

Apart from future CYS or SFHP changes or considerations, the SFHP remains as an important CYS and MH/MR initiative. It has successfully served children and families, explored critical service delivery problems firsthand, and provided a valuable opportunity for SFHP staff members and their counterparts in the private sector and the MH/MR system to discuss the needs of children and families in a fresh, open, and more flexible manner.

REFERENCES

Bryant, B. 1980. *Special foster care: A history and rationale.* Staunton, VA: People Places, Inc.

Carros, T. N. 1984. *Sample Survey, January, 1984 to June, 1984.* Paper presented at meeting of Pennsylvania Children and Youth Administrators, Inc., State College, PA.

Gershenson, C. 1984. The twenty-year trend of federally assisted foster care. Child Welfare Research Notes #8. Washington, DC: Office of Human Development Services, Department of Health and Human Services.

Hawkins, R. P., and Luster, C. 1982. Family-based treatment: A minimally restrictive alternative with special promise. Paper presented in *Behavioral treatment of youth in professional foster homes,* chaired by E. L. Phillips. Symposium presented at the American Psychological Association convention, Washington, DC.

————, and Meadowcroft, P. 1984. *Practical program evaluation in a family-based treatment program for disturbing and disturbed youngsters.* Unpublished manuscripts. Pressley Ridge School, Pittsburgh, PA.

————; ————; Trout, B. A.; and Luster, W. C. 1985. Foster family-based treatment. *Journal of Clinical Child Psychology* 14: 220–228.

Knitzer, J. 1982. *Unclaimed children: The failure of public responsibility to children and adolescents in need of mental health services.* Washington, DC: Children's Defense Fund.

Meadowcroft, P.; Hawkins, R. P.; Trout, B. A.; Grealish, E. M.; and Stark, L. J. 1982. Making family-based treatment accountable: The issue of quality control. Paper presented in *Behavioral treatment of youth in professional foster homes,* chaired by E. L. Phillips. Symposium presented at the American Psychological Association convention, Washington, DC.

III

Two Particular Needs in Therapeutic Foster Care

Introduction to Part 3

I N CHAPTER 1, Robert Hawkins listed seven dimensions along which therapeutic foster care (TFC) programs vary and that appear to be particularly important to their effectiveness as true treatment. One of those dimensions was TFC parent training, another was staff selection and training, and a third was program accountability. Daniel L. Daly's chapter on the training and supervision of treatment parents, in this section, is pertinent to all three. A fourth dimension was the indirect interventions that address the youngster's ecology and his or her fit within it. Anthony Maluccio and James Whittaker's chapter on parent involvement, in this section, is germane to this dimension.

Daly describes various approaches to the issue of whether and how to train treatment parents, pointing out limitations in what is usually done. He describes the responsible approach taken at Boys Town in training "teaching parents" for the 50-some group homes that now constitute the core of their campus program. He also describes the supervision and support given those teaching parents after the initial training.

Daly identifies the hallmarks of their training and supervision, which should assist TFC programs in evaluating their own training and supervision methods. He illustrates parts of the approach concretely, further assisting us in reviewing our own efforts. If TFC programs are to be truly accountable for quality child care and treatment, Daly's descriptions should be taken as advice and heeded.

Maluccio and Whittaker similarly offer sound advice: keep young-sters' parents involved. It is easy to write off one or both of the parents of the disturbed and disturbing youngsters served by most TFC pro-grams, especially when there has been physical or sexual abuse by the parents. But in writing off one abusive parent we often write off a spouse who was not abusive, and we may inadvertently write off siblings, aunts and uncles, cousins, grandparents, and other relatives. This may well be damaging to that family, but, probably more impor-tant to us, it disconnects the very child whom we hope to help from his or her familial roots, from a sense of who he or she is, in part, and where he or she came from. All of us need a sense of belonging, perhaps even a sense of being part of what might be called a family stream that continues across generations, that has a history and a future. We must be especially reluctant to participate in the total removal of a child from his or her family stream.

Our neglect of family involvement is easy to understand. First, we typically are not asked, required, or paid to serve a youngster's family. The youngster is viewed as troubled, not the family system of which he or she is only part; and our role is defined as treating the youngster, almost as though it were a medical problem. Second, it is the youngster with whom we are faced daily, not the family. It is human not to go out and seek further problems to deal with when one is already preoccupied with those staring in one's face. Third, a potent technology of com-prehensive family involvement or intervention is not yet well articulated and evaluated, so it is not widely taught in such disciplines as psycho-logy, social work, or special education.

It is encouraging that of the TFC programs surveyed by Robert Snodgrass and Brad Bryant (in this volume), most offered one or more kinds of service to biological families. How closely these services ap-proximate the types and amounts of involvement that Maluccio and Whittaker would recommend is not clear. For example, we cannot tell to what extent the family is approached as a system (within a com-munity system) rather than as separate individuals each needing treat-ment. Nor can we tell how much parents are encouraged to visit the treatment homes where their child is placed, to what degree effective interpersonal interaction skills are taught, how much rearrangement of physical, social, or economic ecology is carried out, and so on.

Maluccio and Whittaker suggest that the case manager's role, vis-á-vis promoting parent involvement, should be primarily that of a catalyst, so that the parent makes use of existing community resources. While this strategy is consistent with the usual concept of a case manager, alternatives should be considered carefully. Such a strategy can result in services which are inconsistent with one another, too limited to professionals' offices rather than natural environments, too unaccountable for the needed results, too expensive due to high professional fees, and too prone to leave problems unaddressed that the family considers primary [cf. Grealish et al., in press and 1989], and thus lead to client dropout. This, in turn, can lead the case manager to label the family unmotivated. An alternative is for the TFC program to develop its own potential for providing at least all of the frequently-needed services, some in the family's home, others in the home of the treatment family, still others in the office.

REFERENCES

Grealish, E. M.; Hawkins, R. P.; Meadowcroft, P.; and Lynch, P. In press[a]. Serving families of children in therapeutic foster care. In *Troubled youth in treatment homes: Handbook of therapeutic foster care,* edited by P. Meadowcroft, and B. A. Trout. Washington, DC: Child Welfare League of America.

————; ————; ————; Weaver, P.; Frost, S. S.; and McPherson, P. L. 1989. A behavioral group procedure for parents of severely troubled and troubling youths in out-of-home care: Alternative to conventional training. *Child and Youth Care Quarterly* 18:49–61.

Ensuring Quality Child Care and Treatment Through the Program-Specific Skill Training and Supervision of Personnel

DANIEL L. DALY

FOSTER HOME CARE HAS changed dramatically in this century. Foster care has evolved from a system where foster parents provided love and attention to a child's physical needs and, in return, received help in the household or on the family farm [Bryant 1980] into a system where diverse populations of children with special needs (e.g., emotional disturbance, retardation, autism) are offered care *and* treatment [Tovormina et al. 1977].

As foster family service delivery has shifted from providing care to providing care and treatment, demands have concomitantly been placed on programs to provide cost effective services. It is apparent that cost effectiveness can be achieved only if the direct care personnel provide much of the treatment themselves. Care and treatment personnel need the skills to work and live with disturbed and disturbing children. No particular configuration of personality variables guarantee that personnel are competent in care and treatment responsibilities [Ziarnik and Bernstein 1982]. Program directors have learned that only by hiring and/or developing personnel with special skills can their programs hope to provide ethical, effective services.

This paper focuses on the training and supervision of direct child care and treatment personnel. Of course, training and supervision methods and approaches vary widely. Some of these approaches are discussed in this paper and a model is presented that seems especially appropriate for Therapeutic Foster Care (TFC) programs.

Approaches to Initial Training

The initial training of child care personnel and treatment providers ranges from no formal training to the teaching and assessment of specific, technical skills. Some programs have developed their own training or have relied on a combination of university- and agency-provided training courses. Others have proceeded with the belief that child care and treatment skills have to be hired rather than taught. These various practices can be broken down into several approaches. These approaches are characterized, in what follows, in a simplified manner. It should be recognized that most agencies probably use a mixture of approaches in training child care and treatment personnel.

The Natural Skills Approach

Historically, some programs have not incorporated training requirements into personnel selection and development but rely instead on existing skills. A five-state survey of foster care conducted in the 1970s [Vasaly 1976] found that training for foster parents was functionally nonexistent. Foster parent candidates who had experience in child rearing, who seemed emotionally stable and interested in children, and who verbalized values compatible with those of the placing agency were thought to possess the skills necessary for foster parenting. No further training was provided other than exposing the parents to agency policies and operation.

This nontraining approach was consistent with a belief that the professional caseworker, not the foster parents, should be accountable for any decision making. With such an approach, formal training was not essential for direct care providers who were held accountable only for meeting the physical and emotional needs of children. Decisions about what behaviors to teach and how to teach them were apparently either left to the discretion of the foster parent or considered the responsibility of the professionally trained caseworker. In this approach treatment was not the responsibility of foster parents, but, when provided, was the responsibility of a mental health professional.

The University or Lecture Approach

During the 1970s, the child care field as a whole moved in the direction of placing treatment accountability in the hands of direct service providers. There was a growing demand for child care and treatment personnel who had received formal training [Bryant 1980]. Naturally, the most economic process was to hire persons who were already trained. The most readily available training resource was the university system. Courses in social work, psychology, education, and counseling were already in existence and agencies sought to hire persons whom the universities had trained. Programs applying this approach assumed the completion of course work or a degree program qualified a person for service in particular types of programs. The credits, certification, or diploma received symbolized a person's complete readiness to assume certain roles in the human service field. In some instances, personnel with university-based human service training were hired as foster parents in therapeutic or specialized foster care programs [Bryant 1980].

However, the typical college program does not prepare personnel for roles in TFC programs. For one thing, the university or lecture approach used in most degree programs is predominantly a conceptual/verbal one. Conceptual/verbal training does not necessarily generalize to improved on-the-job performance. Readings and lectures are the primary input to trainees in this approach, which assumes that most conceptual mastery will translate into the implementation of specific skills. Of course, some practical experience is included in university-based human service training, but it is usually a rather modest fraction of the training. Furthermore, practical experience training is more difficult to evaluate and seldom conducted so thoroughly that the faculty can say with certainty that a student has mastered specific skills.

The strength of the university or lecture approach is the development of a general, conceptual/verbal base that prepares trainees to communicate and understand a wide range of issues in human service. The weakness of this approach is that most curricula below the master's degree level do not prepare the student for child care activities that require specific behavioral skills. The stimulus situation in traditional undergraduate curricula more closely approximates academic than work situations and the behaviors required are primarily verbal. Masters' or doctoral programs are more likely to prepare students to perform specific skills such as psychotherapy or staff consultation, provided they include several different practice and clerkship experiences to develop and access the skills necessary for jobs in the field. Undergraduate degree programs rarely have practice or clerkship experiences that directly prepare personnel for the role of therapeutic foster parents.

The Preservice/Inservice Approach

Many human service agencies develop their own training programs in the form of preservice or inservice training. Either by conducting the training themselves or by contracting it to outside experts, agencies attempt to promote philosophical and operational consistency and quality within their programs. This is the type of training model that dominates the training of educators. Educators are provided with annual inservice training for which they are granted continuing education credits. A crucial weakness of the preservice/inservice approach is that it is traditionally not followed up by systematic, performance-based feedback [Quilitch 1975]. Preservice/inservice training results in small changes in behavior immediately after training but, without performance-based feedback, only inconsistently translates to improved performance on the job [Ziarnik and Bernstein 1982]. Many programs model this approach—mandating annual training credits to obtain or maintain licensure, but failing to followup with systematic, on-the-job feedback.

The conceptual/verbal approach predominates this type of training, with training being about some behavior change technology or interpersonal relationship rather than what to do. Training often consists of lectures, readings, and discussions that provide information about child care and treatment practices but often do not translate into what staff members should do differently on the job. It is hoped that because people have heard about new ideas or skills they can translate them into improved job functioning. Furthermore, there often is no attempt to evaluate what skills are actually learned in such training experiences. If there is evaluation of the training, it may take the form of consumer satisfaction questionnaires or paper or pencil tests that measure cognitive skills—neither of which is likely to assess to what extent new, on-the-job skills were learned. There is no conclusive evidence that happy trainees or increased cognitive understanding will translate to improved skills in the workplace [Ziarnik and Bernstein 1982].

The Program-Specific Skills Approach

The program-specific skills approach emphasizes the development of specific behavioral skills (versus only conceptual knowledge) that the designers of the program have selected as particularly significant. These are skills that make up a large part of the care and treatment behaviors desired of personnel. This approach to training attempts to teach personnel what to do in performing their job rather than only about performing their job. Here the effort is to minimize theory and general concepts and to approximate as closely as possible the more challenging stimulus situations that will be faced on the job. For instance, more training time is given to watching skills modeled by live or videotaped models and actually practicing the skills than to reading about or listening to lectures about child care skills. The greatest percentage of training time may be devoted to behavioral rehearsal where trainees practice desired skills in situations that closely approximate those on the job. These techniques have been demonstrated to be more effective than conceptual/verbal approaches in developing personnel skills [Delamater et al. 1984].

Further, the skills taught are ones that have been chosen as a high priority by those responsible for developing the program. This requires considerable expertise of the developers and a willingness to make a commitment as to what is important. This commitment needs to be open to revision based upon program experience and evaluation combined with advances of knowledge and technology in behavior science [Hawkins et al. 1985]. What is chosen as high priority should be influenced by such factors as the existing skills of program personnel, legal and regulatory requirements, the magnitude of benefits likely to accrue to children or their families by use of the skills, the risks involved in the misuse of the particular skills, and the skills of the supervisory personnel who have the responsibility for assuring consistent implementation on the job.

Another major component of the program-specific skills approach is the evaluation of trainee learning. As noted, evaluation is often neglected in conceptual/verbal approaches; and in those instances when it is conducted, only conceptual/verbal knowledge is often measured. In the skills-oriented approach, evaluation should always be conducted to assess to what extent specific behavioral skills have been learned, using such methods as the analog assessment of behavior rehearsal or role play [Goldsmith and McFall 1975]. Written or oral tests may augment, but not replace, actual demonstration of learned behaviors in the skills-oriented approach.

Approaches to Supervision and Support

Analogous to the variety of approaches to initial training, there are various models of supervision ranging from little or no direction, monitoring, or feedback, to structured, systematic guidance and evaluation. Supervision is intended to augment initial training and feedback so that staff skills may be further refined and developed to optimize consistent implementation of the planned program, and to motivate personnel so that they remain enthusiastic and creative in their roles. Like training, supervision methods can be classified into several approaches, admittedly oversimplified to highlight their differences.

Laissez-Faire Approach

In this approach, there is little specific direction or proactive guidance given by supervisors or consultants. Once hired, personnel are basically left on their own in the day-to-day operation of their program. No clear criteria are established to mark good performance and personnel are assumed to be performing adequately as long as they do not commit a serious error.

An obvious weakness of this approach is that staff members may not know what an error is until it has been made. Less obvious, but more pervasively damaging, is the absence of accountability procedures that promote high-quality service. Thus, service tends to decline to the lowest tolerable level of quality. When it is provided, adequate supervision is measured by number of hours rather than by the skills implementation of the personnel and corresponding improvement in the development of the child. In an environment where staff members do not clearly understand the expectations for good performance, supervisors do not systematically monitor, and differential consequences do not follow differential performance quality, it is unlikely that high quality service and enthusiastic, energetic performance will be maintained.

The Heads-Will-Roll Approach

This approach to supervision is easily identified in the business world, but also exists in child care and treatment programs. In this approach, heads will roll if certain procedural or undesired outcomes occur. For instance, a child might be removed from placement in a foster home in which abusive discipline practices occur or in which inadequate school attendance is maintained.

This approach is better than the laissez-faire approach in that there are at least some well-defined objectives and contingencies. It produces greater accountability because consequences are more consistently paired with either the failure to attain some objective or the misuse of some procedure. It also may improve upon the laissez-faire approach by providing inservice training and consultation.

A major weakness of this approach is that it places emphasis on the avoidance of certain errors or outcomes rather than the active implementation of good procedures and the attainment of desirable outcomes. As such, it is likely to motivate those caring for children to avoid making major errors, but it is less likely to promote desirable, proactive child-caring skills.

The Specify, Teach, Support, and Evaluate (STSE) Approach

In the STSE approach, supervision is conducted in a highly structured, specific format. Programs employing this approach have well-specified training, consultation, and evaluation components that are integrated into a total training and supervision model [Peter 1986]. These programs use the program specific-skills approach in training and follow this up with systematic supervision that continually defines the role of those providing child care.

The STSE approach differs from both the laissez-faire approach and the typical heads-will-roll approach in that specific, continual supervision is provided. It is similar to the heads-will-roll approach in that consequences are paired with performance, but different in that this approach also pairs positive consequences with correct program implementation.

The degree of structure and specification of job performance is far greater than in the other two approaches. Personnel are assigned a supervisor who is available continually to them—even on a 24-hour basis—and makes regular visits at the worksite to observe, teach, and help solve problems. Personnel are provided with other forms of programmatic support in terms of procedural checklists [Reflections of Current Youth Care Practices 1979], youth skills curricula [Baron et al. 1976] and an evaluation system that gives detailed feedback on how they are performing their child care and treatment tasks [Daly et al. 1982]. Although the expectations for total performance are likely to be higher in this approach, heads rarely roll because the program is specified well enough so that the desired behaviors can be performed without strain or loss of enthusiasm.

Evaluation in the STSE method is employed to ensure that the skills learned in the training and consultation components are truly used in program operation [Daly and Daly 1977]. Many programs have failed because program technology was never employed or employed improperly [Brendtro and Ness 1982]. In one documented case [Patton 1978], a state legislature terminated all funding for welfare recipients' training because a hastily conducted outcome evaluation indicated that the program had no measurable impact. Subsequent inquiry into the reasons for the program's ineffectiveness indicated that the program had, in fact, never been implemented.

The Boys Town Family Home Program (BTFHP) [Peter 1986] has been a major stimulus in the development of approaches to the training and supervision of personnel for child care and treatment. It is appropriate to examine the BTFHP program when discussing TFC programs. It includes and expands upon the procedural underpinnings of TFC programs discussed in Hampson [1988]—namely that staff members be specially selected and trained; children and staff members be matched; high-intensity and high-frequency casework services be offered; and direct care personnel be afforded professional status.

The BTFHP is a family-based program staffed by a specially selected, full-time married couple known as Family-Teachers. The Family-Teachers live with a small number of children, and their role is the individualized care and treatment of children with behavior and emotional problems. The BTFHP approaches training, supervision, and support in a comprehensive, broadbased fashion, employing preservice training, inservice training, ongoing consultation, and performance evaluation. The Family-Teachers leave an assigned consultant (caseworker) available on a 24-hour basis. The Family-Teachers are designated as the primary treatment personnel and receive organizational, social, and monetary status that defines their role as professionals. This model integrates the program-specific skills approach to training and the STSE approach to supervision into a system or model whose goal is to promote optimal staff performance.

TFC programs like People Places [Snodgrass and Campbell 1981]; Professional Parenting [Timbers et al. 1982]; and PRYDE [Meadowcroft et al. 1982] use similar training and supervision technology in their foster care and treatment programs. The technology works well in group homes and these TFC homes because the program planners subscribe to many of the same program philosophies and goals, with common properties or hallmarks.

Hallmarks of an Effective Training and Supervision Model

Effective training and supervision models have in common certain qualities or hallmarks:

1. The program goals are clearly identified.

2. The program is well defined.

3. The program procedures relate clearly to program goals.

4. The personnel training and education methods ensure learning.

5. The personnel supervision methods ensure program implementation.

6. The personnel supervision methods result in continued program refinement.

7. The personnel education and supervision methods shape the overall program culture.

Hallmark #1—The Program Goals Are Clearly Identified

Program goals are the starting point in the development of all program support systems. For instance, a program goal to provide a family-style environment generates decisions affecting staffing, facilities, training, consultation, and evaluation.

The stated goals in the BTFHP [Daly et al. 1984] are to provide care that is humane, effective, satisfactory to its participants, cost effective, and replicable. These goals are the focal points in the development of training, consultation, evaluation, and administrative services. The third goal, that of providing care that is satisfactory to participants, has generated not only personnel training procedures intended to develop skills related to consumer satisfaction, but also evaluation procedures to assess attainment of this goal.

The more clearly that program goals and objectives are specified, the easier is the task of defining program procedures. The following questions must be answered in specifying program procedures: What kind of children will be served? What are the referral problems? What environment will the children live in? What will be their opportunities, responsibilities, and restrictions? How long should children be in the program? What staff behaviors are necessary to serve the children? How can staff members be taught these behaviors? How can implementation be ensured?

Specifying program goals makes it possible to then define the nature of the program. For instance, if a program has a goal to provide humane care (i.e., one that protects and promotes the rights of children), program components can be specified to accomplish the goal—such as designing a training workshop that defines children's rights and teaches procedures to ensure their protection. A series of workshop sections related to the goal of providing humane care can be formulatd. A consultation or casework component can be initiated that both permits program supervisors to observe the level of implementation of humane care procedures and also provides a process for remediating deficiencies in implementation. And, finally, an evaluation component can be built that monitors the effects of humane care.

Hallmark #2—The Program Is Well Defined

A well-defined program comprises ·behavioral units that can be taught, observed, retaught, and measured [Mager and Pipe 1970]. Program planners define what skills are needed by the staff. Trainers know what skills to teach, consultants and caseworkers know what skills to observe, and evaluators know what skills to evaluate.

An example of a well-defined program component used in the Boys Town Family Home Program is the "teaching interaction" [Phillips et al. 1974]. The teaching interaction is a step-by-step process used by Boys Town Family-Teachers to teach new skills to children or to change inappropriate behaviors into more appropriate behaviors. The teaching interaction is operationalized to the extent that it can be taught, learned, observed, and evaluated. The basic components of a teaching interaction are presented in figure 1. The adult behaviors in the teaching interaction are related to the goals of providing humane care (praise and rationales) and effective care (role playing and consequences) [Bedlington et al. 1978]. Research has shown that the teaching interaction is also related to care that is satisfactory to its child participants [Willner et al. 1977]. The teaching interaction in complete or abbreviated form is one of the major care and treatment components employed by Family-Teachers in the BTFHP.

Hallmark #3—The Program Procedures Relate Clearly to Program Objectives

Once program objectives are clearly defined, procedures can be developed that relate to attainment of the objectives. The BTFHP exemplifies how program goals generate program procedures. Some objectives of the BTFHP are:

to provide long-term, family-style care for placed children

to ensure that each child's rights are protected

to effect change in referral problem behaviors

to promote academic growth

Each of these objectives generates specific content areas in the preservice training program. For instance, the objective of providing long-term (i.e., more than six months), family-style care for seriously disturbed and disturbing children necessitates the development of several relevant skills. Family-Teachers need to know how to interact with the child (i.e., how to interact effectively, when to interact, how to integrate this child into their own family, and how to help their family effectively make the necessary life-style adjustments created by a new family member), and also how to work with school systems and other community resources that can have a favorable or unfavorable effect on the child's length of treatment.

These are only a few of the skills needed to achieve just one objective of the program. Training provided in the preservice and inservice workshop sections must cover a wide array of topics to ensure that Family-Teachers have the content necessary to achieve the objective. The Boys Town program [Boys Town Family Home Training Manual 1986] contains workshop sections such as Relationship Building, Child Health Care, Promoting Family Environments, Family De-

Teaching Interaction Component	Example	Rationale for the component
1. Expression of affection (a smile, friendly greeting, joke, or physical contact)	Family-Teacher smiles and greets "Hi. How is it going?" He puts his hand on the child's back.	Signals to the child that the Family-Teacher is pleased to see him and likes to interact with him.
2. Praise for what has been accomplished	"You have done a nice job of picking up your room."	Shows the child that the Family-Teacher notices what he has accomplished.
3. Description of the inappropriate behavior	"Your bed is wrinkled."	Instructs the youth about what he did incorrectly or hasn't yet done.
4. Description of the appropriate behavior	"A bed looks much neater when the spread is flat and tucked in at the bottom." (Family-Teacher points.) "Let me show you how to make a bed." (Family-Teacher demonstrates.)	Instructs the youth about what is expected of him. The task often should be broken into small steps. Demonstration may be needed in order to clarify the verbal instruction.
5. Rationale for the appropriate behavior	"A neatly made bed is more comfortable to sleep in. Also, a neatly made bed makes your whole room look nicer."	Instructs the youth in the personal benefits for engaging in the behaviors.

6. Request for acknowledgment	"Do you understand?"	Allows the youth to ask any questions he may have. Also, the youth's acknowledgment signals to the Family-Teacher that the youth was attending and understands the instructions.
7. Practice	"Now you make up your bed without wrinkles?"	Practice is very important. It shows the Family-Teacher whether or not the youth knows the new behaviors and gives the youth a chance to practice.
8. Feedback during practice	"That looks good. Now don't forget to tuck the spread in at the bottom. Good job!"	Gives positive feedback for behavior performed correctly and gives the youth additional practice on behaviors not yet a part of his repertoire.
9. Reward: Praise and points	"Give yourself 1,500 points. You did a good job on your bed."	Gives the youth immediate consequences for the appropriate behavior.

*Reprinted with permission from the Boys Town Family Home Program training manual. (1986) Boys Town, NE: Father Flanagan's Boys' Home.

*Figure 1—The Teaching Interaction**

143

cision Making, and Working with Natural Parents—all related to the objective of providing long-term, family-style care.

Only after the objectives are specified can procedures like the sections in the training program be established. Each program must customize its training content to fit its own established objectives. Objectives will differ depending upon the clients, personnel configuration, treatment setting, and so on.

Hallmark #4—The Personnel Training and Education Methods Ensure Learning

As discussed in hallmark #2, specifying program components makes them considerably easier to teach, but the teaching methods are equally important in determining how well they are learned. A general rule of thumb is to employ teaching methods and training materials that approximate the actual job situation. Most of the skills demanded in TFC programs are interaction skills. Therapeutic Foster Parents interact with children, with the parents of children, with agency workers, with teachers, and with neighbors. During training the trainees should be given many opportunities to practice the same kind of interactions they will face with these individuals when in the mode of a Family-Teacher or foster parent.

The workshop process needs to be designed so that skill modeling and practice time are maximized [Delamater et al. 1984]. Lectures and readings are important for trainees because they develop conceptual skills, but actual behavioral proficiency is more likely to be developed by skill modeling and repeated practice with feedback in between. The preservice training for Family-Teachers at Boys Town allots 75% of a workshop section for the modeling and role playing of the skills that constitute the teaching interaction.

One way to provide trainees with skill modeling is to employ videotaped "wrong way/right way" models—a form of discrimination training. Video examples of situations that trainees will face on the job are presented, with models depicting both inappropriate and appropriate use of program procedures. These videotapes generally follow brief lecture sessions and visually highlight the lecture content. It is best if trainees are individually required to judge the performance seen from the tape before they hear the trainer's judgments. In this way they learn the critical features of the performance.

An effective way to provide trainees with opportunities to practice program skills is to use behavioral rehearsals or program simulations employing youth confederates (persons trained to play simulated child roles). Situations requiring trainees to praise, give criticism, teach new skills, provide positive or negative consequences, and calm an out-of-control child can be presented. Actually acting out these often new behaviors not only is the most effective way to enable learning or memory of the behaviors to occur, but also the supportive feedback from the trainer allows the trainee to gain confidence in his or her ability to produce the behavior when needed.

Training methodology is important because it is related to the desired outcome of personnel acquiring skill mastery. The critical question in any training program is whether the skills are learned. Two of the more popular methods of assessing learning are pre-post verbal simulations with verbal answers and pre-post behavioral vignettes.

In the verbal simulations, personnel are presented with a description of a situation they are likely to face in the home, and they produce a verbal response describing what program components they would employ in such a situation. This type of measure assesses gains in verbal understanding of the program, but it does not assess the ability to use the skills appropriately or at appropriate times. Sometimes trainees are required not only to describe what they would do, but why. This assesses their conceptual/verbal rationales for procedures and can be useful in developing their skills in explaining the program to consumers such as biological parents or teachers.

The pre-post behavioral simulation is a more direct and realistic measure of the skill mastery of trainees. In this procedure, trainees are presented with similar situations both pretraining and posttraining, and are required to show how they would use the program. Their responses are then evaluated, perhaps with a checklist of skill components. This information provides trainers, supervisors, and trainees with precise information for remediating any skill deficits of current or prospective personnel. Also, it provides trainers with an assessment of training methods. An interesting benefit of such a precise, criterion-based evaluation is that trainees are frequently more motivated to be present and attentive when they know that there will be some post-workshop assessment of their skills.

Hallmark #5—The Personnel Supervision Methods Ensure Program Implementation

In many TFC programs and in the Boys Town Family Home Program, the definition of training has been expanded to include not only traditional preservice/inservice training components but also consultation and evaluation components. Training is viewed as a continuing process that lasts throughout the involvement of personnel with the program. Preservice workshops merely initiate the learning experience. Learning continues with in-home training via an assigned consultant and through feedback provided by regular evaluations. Consultation and evaluation provide continuing consistent performance feedback to personnel on program implementation. In their review of child care personnel management strategies, Reid and Whitman [1983] conclude that performance feedback and "multifaceted" intervention (i.e., training, performance feedback, evaluation) are more likely to effect program implementation than are antecedent strategies such as preservice training alone. Data collected via consultation or evaluation may indicate remediation in the form of retaking workshop sections or further in-home training [Hawkins et al. 1985].

In the cited TFC programs, three basic components are involved in the ongoing training or supervision process: consultation, procedural manuals, and evaluation. All three components are closely tied to the content of the preservice workshops. The consultation component provides in-home training of the workshop skills. The procedural manuals serve as cues that enhance routine skill implementation. The evaluation component provides feedback on the implementation of the skills taught and described in the manuals; and, when tied to incentives such as pay increases and continued employment, evaluation maintains motivation to use the skills.

Consultation.   Child care personnel are assigned a consultant who is available on a 24-hour basis. The consultants provide advice, support, and direction through regularly scheduled meetings, phone contacts, and emergency contacts as needed. Most meetings occur at the home of the child care personnel. Sometimes the consultants offer advice on how to prevent or handle a problem, sometimes they simply praise the accomplishments of personnel or provide empathy and understanding for difficulties or perceived failures. The consultants have in-depth knowledge of each child because they participate in the parent-child matching and the development of the individual treatment plan.

Direct observation, in-home retraining, and daily records are three aspects of consultation that are most likely to ensure program implementation [Boys Town Consultant Training Manual 1988]. A consultant tries to maximize in-home observation contact. This provides an opportunity to see not only the child's behavior but also how well the TFC parents are using the program [Smart et al. 1980]. Feedback, and in some cases, modeling and further rehearsal are used for any needed retraining of TFC parents in the use of various program procedures.

Daily records such as the LODE in the PRYDE program [Hawkins et al. 1985; Meadowcroft et al. 1982] and the point card at Boys Town [Boys Town Family Home Program Training Manual 1986] also help the consultant to assess program usage. These records give consultants a snapshot of TFC parent-child interactions, what child behaviors are occurring, and how well treatment procedures are being implemented. Praise or retraining of the TFC parents can be given by the consultant based upon the data from these records.

Procedural Manuals.   Manuals serve as a cue to enhance program implementation. Checklists itemizing program procedures to use in response to child runaways, drug or alcohol use, or medical emergencies [*Reflections of Current Youth Care Practices* 1979] are provided to parents as an aid or reference source. They assist consultants or supervisors in reviewing what was done by child care personnel, thus helping to standardize program use during special or crisis situations. Phone or direct contact consultation is available, but manuals help child care personnel to implement many procedures without personal consultation. Figure 2 contains a sample procedural checklist.

Evaluation.   The evaluation component is the most easily identified quality-control component. Performance on evaluation can be paired with pay incentives and an annual certification that recognizes personnel who have provided quality services for their children. If personnel are recruited with the understanding that routine evaluation is an integral part of their job as TFC parents, and if their training and supervision are adequate, the evaluation should not be an occasion for high anxiety or resentment. If, in addition, routine consultation activities and unofficial evaluations are made available as preparation, personnel should not only perform well on evaluations, but more importantly, should perform optimally in their work with children and program consumers. Both Boys Town Family-Teachers and PRYDE Treatment Parents receive a six-month and a 12-month certification evaluation in their first year, with annual certification evaluations occurring subsequently.

At Boys Town and at PRYDE, three basic areas are assessed on

Introduction

Working with a youth who has a runaway problem requires a great deal of patience and concern on the part of the Family-Teachers. While the youth is away from the Family-Teachers' care, the youth could experience many dangerous and disastrous events. The primary concern of the Family-Teachers should always be to locate the youth to assure his/her safety. (Note: Be aware that the term "running away" may be a misnomer, and in the Family-Teacher's analysis of the cause of the situation, the fact that the youth may be "running to" something may need to be considered.)

Purpose

The purpose of this procedure is to familiarize the Family-Teachers with some steps to be taken in the event that a youth runs away. This procedure should not only aid in quicker location of the youth, but also help to discourage this kind of behavior as a solution to problems.

Prevention

Although there is a high correlation between "good weather" and running away, there are several preventative measures that Family-Teachers can provide in order to lessen the frequency with which a youth would run away. The Family-Teachers should provide a pleasant place for the child to live both physically as well as socially, including showing concern and understanding. Preventatively teaching alternatives to problem behaviors of the youth such as ability to take criticism, ability to respond to the word "no" or negative consequences, ability to be appropriately assertive, decrease the frequency of conflict situations. Counseling about running away and alternatives help if youth has just experienced a large negative consequence. Do not "push" the youth, but do not fail to "teach" and "discipline."

Definition

A suggested definition for a runaway is: any youth whom the Family-Teachers have reason to believe has left without permission and does not plan to return that same day.

Procedure

___ A.. At the time the youth is suspected of being absent, check extensively with the other youths in your home, the youth's friends, and the youth's "hangouts" in an effort to locate him/her.

___ B. If the youth is unaccounted for:

_____ 1. Recheck by phone the areas where the youth was supposed to have been or the persons the youth was supposed to have been with.

_____ 2. Notify your Community Director.

_____ 3. Contact the Boys Town Police Department at Ext. 1171 for notification and request that they notify the youth's home community police and sheriff's department as well as local police and sheriff's departments after 24 hours have elapsed.

_____ 4. Contact the parent(s), guardian(s), and/or agency(ies), social welfare, probation officer, etc., who have co-responsibility for the youth.

_____ 5. Contact the principal of the appropriate school.

_____ 6. Check local hospitals. The Douglas County Sheriff's Office and Omaha Police do not contact area hospitals to check on runaways. The chances are slim that the youth would be admitted to a hospital without that hospital contacting the Home, unless the youth would not or could not relay the information.

_____ C. Upon the youth's return you should welcome him/her back into your home.

_____ 1. Praise the youth for returning home.

_____ 2. Attend to immediate physical needs such as food and cleanliness.

_____ 3. Attempt to determine if the youth has endangered himself/herself by sexual or illegal behavior while on runaway status.

_____ D. After the youth has returned or you have located the youth and determined his/her condition:

_____ 1. Notify the Community Director and submit another Home Report containing what occurred and what your response will be.

_____ 2. Notify the youth's parent(s) or guardian(s).

_____ 3. Notify the Boys Town Police Department.

_____ 4. Deliver the appropriate consequences.

_____ 5. Bring the issue up for discussions at Family Conference.

*Reprinted with permission from *Reflections of current youth care practices* (1979). Boys Town, NE: Father Flanagan's Boys' Home.

Figure 2—Youth Runaway Procedure *

149

each evaluation. These are program implementation, consumer satisfaction, and program effectiveness. The program implementation area relates directly to how well the personnel are using the program as learned in the workshop, consultation, and procedural manuals. In-home evaluation visits are used both at Boys Town and PRYDE to assess program implementation directly. Critical program components such as teaching interactions or the use of a token economy are observed by evaluators who rate these skills. Child care personnel are provided with an evaluation write-up containing the evaluation data and recommendations for skill improvement.

The consumer evaluations assess the level of satisfaction of the children with the program as well as the satisfaction of other consumers such as teachers and the agencies that placed the child. These consumers provide indirect assessment of skills taught in the training program. Their summarized scores and comments are provided to the Family-Teachers along with evaluator recommendations for further development in working with consumers. Figure 3 presents a youth consumer evaluation conducted in a face-to-face interview with each Boys Town youth. Figure 4 contains an evaluation form that is sent to all social agencies that place youths at Boys Town. Criterion scores are 6.0 on a seven-point rating scale. An average score of 6.0 must be reached for all consumer groups.

At Boys Town, program effectiveness is assessed in a variety of ways during treatment and posttreatment measures [Phillips et al. 1981]. This information is used as an indirect measure of program implementation and a direct measure of program goal attainment. The type of information collected is derived from the program goal to provide effective care—effective in improving school performance or in reducing delinquent behavior or status offenses.

In TFC programs many goals might be the basis for evaluating program effectiveness. For example, it is generally desirable that a youth not move from one home to another. Placement stability can be assessed by measuring the percentage of youths retained by a single treatment home or by the number of in-program transfers made per child until a successful discharge. Another, more individualized, measure of effectiveness is the youth's progress on behaviors that originally led to placement, such as verbal or physical aggression, running away, or truancy. Data on school performance or property destruction might also be kept. The data reflect the extent to which the environment provided by the child care personnel produces behavior change, the primary purpose of the treatment program. The data can not only be used to evaluate programs as a whole, but also, if individual youth baselines are kept, to evaluate the performance of child care personnel [Hawkins et al. 1982].

Hallmark #6—The Personnel Supervision Methods Result in Continued Program Refinement

Another hallmark of an effective training and supervision process is the capability to stimulate program growth and development. This is facilitated in the program under discussion by the nature of the consultation and evaluation processes. The nature of the supervision—its frequency, reliance on data, and its flexibility—allows for program refinement at all levels.

Consultation and evaluation data are useful in answering many questions about program implementation. Which components do the child care personnel and children feel are most effective? What successful adaptations to procedures have child care personnel or supervisors made? Is the program being implemented? Which components are less adequately implemented or impractical to implement? Which components facilitate family-based treatment? Which components hinder family-based care? This information helps program planners to modify program procedures as they are taught in workshops, consultation, and manuals.

Consultation and evaluation data are useful in assessing the achievement of program goals. Are the children happy? Are they progressing in school? Are stable placements being established? Are children's rights being respected? Are there changes in referral problem behaviors? Which behaviors? When answers to questions such as these are in the desired direction, program planners have some level of comfort with program quality. When answers are in a less desired direction, remediation can take place for individual child care personnel, consultants, trainers, or in the program design itself.

Finally, program implementation information is useful in relating the program procedures to outcomes. When there is evidence that the program is implemented, valid conclusions relating the program to outcomes can be made [Hawkins et al. 1982]. This helps to build

Family-Teachers _____ Date _____

Evaluation Type _____

1. How satisfied are you that _____ and _____ try to be fair when you earn and lose points and privileges?
    ___ Rating   Comment:

2. How satisfied are you that _____ and _____ have clearly explained what skills you are expected to learn in order to complete the program?
    ___ Rating   Comment:

3. How satisfied are you that you have a chance to express your own ideas, ask questions, and help make decisions about the treatment program?
    ___ Rating   Comment:

4. How satisfied are you that, if you want to, you can talk with _____ and _____ about problems you may have?
    ___ Rating   Comment:

5. How satisfied are you that _____ and _____ care about you and your success in the future?
    ___ Rating   Comment:

6. How satisfied are you that _____ and _____ have been able to teach you important skills such as how to accept criticism, how to follow instructions, how to get along with other people, how to care for your belongings, and good study habits?
    ___ Rating   Comment:

7. How satisfied are you that _____ and _____ are teaching skills that will help you when you leave the program?
    ___ Rating   Comment:

8. How satisfied are you that _____ and _____ are usually pleasant?
    ___ Rating   Comment:

152

9. How satisfied are you that _____ and _____ teach all the youth in your home to be pleasant toward each other?
_____ Rating   Comment:

10. How satisfied are you that _____ and _____ are trying to help you get along better with your parents?
_____ Rating   Comment:

11. How satisfied are you that _____ and _____ are trying to help you get along better with your teachers?
_____ Rating   Comment:

12. How satisfied are you that _____ and _____ try to help you do your best to learn and benefit from this program?
_____ Rating   Comment:

13. How satisfied are you with this treatment program as compared with others (e.g., training school, therapeutic camps, etc.) in which you have participated or about which you have heard?
_____ Rating   Comment:

14. Are there any changes or improvements you think should be made in the program?
_____ Rating   Comment:

Youth ratings use a seven point satisfaction scale with number corresponding to these verbal descriptions:

1=completely dissatisfied   5=slightly satisfied
2=dissatisfied   6=satisfied
3=slightly dissatisfied   7=completely satisfied
4=neither satisfied nor dissatisfied

* Reprinted with permission from the *Boys Town evaluation training manual: A handbook for professional evaluators.* (1987) Boys Town, NE: Father Flanagan's Boys' Home

*Figure 3—Youth Consumer Evaluation**

Family-Teacher(s) _____ Youth _____

Address _____ Date _____

1. Are you satisfied that the Family-Teachers are doing an effective job of correcting the problems of this youth who has been placed in their care?

Comments

____ Completely satisfied _____

____ Satisfied _____

____ Slightly satisfied _____

____ Neither satisfied nor dissatisfied _____

____ Slightly dissatisfied _____

____ Dissatisfied _____

____ Completely dissatisfied _____

2. Are you satisfied with the amount of cooperation you have received from the Family-Teachers in their interactions with your Agency concerning this youth?

Comments

____ Completely satisfied _____

____ Satisfied _____

____ Slightly satisfied _____

____ Neither satisfied nor dissatisfied _____

____ Slightly dissatisfied _____

____ Dissatisfied _____

____ Completely dissatisfied _____

3. Are you satisfied with the level of communication you have had with the Family-Teachers concerning this youth?

Comments

_____ Completely satisfied

_____ Satisfied

_____ Slightly satisfied

_____ Neither satisfied nor dissatisfied

_____ Slightly dissatisfied

_____ Dissatisfied

_____ Completely dissatisfied

4. Are you satisfied with the pleasantness of interactions you have had with the Family-Teachers?

Comments

_____ Completely satisfied

_____ Satisfied

_____ Slightly satisfied

_____ Neither satisfied nor dissatisfied

_____ Slightly dissatisfied

_____ Dissatisfied

_____ Completely dissatisfied

5. Any comments, suggestions, or additional information concerning the Family-Teachers or their home would be appreciated.

*Reprinted with permission form the Boys Town evaluation training manual: A handbook for professional evaluators. (1987). Boys Town, NE: Father Flanagan's Boys' Home

Figure 4
*Social Agency Evaluation Form**

155

information not only on the program itself but for the child care and treatment field at large.

Hallmark #7—The Personnel Education and Supervision Methods Shape the Overall Program Culture

The book *Corporate Cultures* [Deal and Kennedy 1982] carries the message that strong cultures make strong companies. The authors contend that the values, rights, rituals, and models of a company are just as important as the procedural aspects of corporate management. This is also consistent with the finding of Peters and Waterman [1982] from their study of 62 unusually well-managed companies.

Similarly, an effective training and supervision process develops a strong culture in a child care and treatment program. How these processes operate is as important to the success of a program as what is in the training. Via their interactions with trainers, consultants, and evaluators, child care personnel learn program values and philosophy. The culture shapes personnel behaviorally, emotionally, and conceptually. This in turn affects how they operate their homes, how they describe the program, and how they interact with consumers.

As previously mentioned, the teaching interaction process (see figure 1) is a basic component in the BTFHP. This teaching interaction process is also used by trainers, consultants, and evaluators in their interactions with the staff. As a result, praise for approximations and effort, compassionate explanation, supportive skill building, and free flow of information are values that are likely to become part of a program that incorporates the teaching interaction into all of its units.

Similarly, the emphasis on evaluation in modifying program design, developing workshop and consultation components, defining child care personnel roles—all with the goal of providing the best quality care for children—will affect the program culture. An open program, unthreatened by the gaze of observers, is the likely result.

Consider some of the program values that are likely to be developed by the training and supervision process described here. Personnel are exposed to a training process that emphasizes positive reinforcement, individualization, consistency, attention to detail, the importance of feedback, the importance of child and consumer happiness, and data-based decision making. Child care personnel are likely to mirror these values in their operation of their home, and their children will benefit.

Conclusion

Child care and treatment programs need to expand their definitions of what constitutes adequate personnel preparation. The traditional practice of teaching skills without creating contingencies that prompt and motivate personnel to use them is inadequate. Many programs have failed, not because they were poorly planned, but because they were poorly implemented.

Child-caring professionals have always desired quality care, but the motivation to provide quality care is not enough to ensure it. The past decade has seen the development of programs and procedures that now permit us to close the gap between mere espousal of goals and their actual achievement. The task now is to commit the effort and resources necessary to build these procedures into the training and supervision processes used by child care staff and treatment programs.

REFERENCES

Baron, R. L.; Cunningham, P. J.; Palma, L. J.; and Phillips, E. L. 1976. *Family and community living skills curriculum*. Boys Town, NE: Father Flanagan's Boys' Home.

Bedlington, M. M.; Solnick, J. V.; Schumaker, J. B.; Braukmann, C. J.; Kirigin, J. A.; and Wolf, M. M. 1978. Paper presented at the American Psychological Association convention, Toronto.

Brentro, L. K., and Ness, A. E. 1982. Perspectives on peer group treatment: The use and abuse of guided group interaction/positive peer culture. *Children and Youth Services Review* 4: 307–324.

Boys Town consultant training manual. 1988. Boys Town, NE: Father Flanagan's Boys' Home.

Boys Town evaluation training manual: A handbook for professional evaluators. 3rd ed. 1987. Boys Town, NE: Father Flanagan's Boys' Home.

Boys Town Family Home Program training manual. 1986. Boys Town, NE: Father Flanagan's Boys' Home.

Bryant, B. 1980. *Special foster care: A History and Rationale*. Verona, VA: People Places, Inc.

Daly, D. L.; Coughlin, D. D.; and Baron, R. L. 1984. The Boys Town Family Home Program. *Speaking for Children* 3: Lincoln, NE: The Junior League of Nebraska.

———, and Daly, P. B. 1977. *Quality controls for institutional programs*. Paper presented at American Psychological Association Convention, San Francisco, CA.

Daly, P. B.; Wineman, J. H.; Daly, D. L.; and Luger, R. L. 1982. Evaluation of staff performance. In *Practical program evaluation in youth treatment,* edited by A. J. McSweeny, W. J. Fremouw, and R. P. Hawkins, 144–163. Springfield, IL: Charles C. Thomas.

Deal, T. E., and Kennedy, A. A. 1982. *Corporate cultures.* London: Addison-Wesley.

Delamater, A. M.; Conners, C. K.; and Wells, K. C. 1984. A comparison of staff training procedures: Behavioral application in the child psychiatric inpatient setting. *Behavior Modification* 8 (1): 39–58.

Goldsmith, J. B., and McFall, R. M. 1975. Development and evaluation of an interpersonal skills training program for psychiatric inpatients. *Journal of Abnormal Psychology* 84 (1): 51–58.

Hampson, R. B. 1988. Special foster care for exceptional children: A review of programs and policies: *Children and Youth Services Review* 10: 19–41.

Hawkins, R. P.; Meadowcroft, P.; Trout, B. A.; and Luster, W. C. (1985). Foster family-based treatment. *Journal of Clinical Child Psychology* 14: 220–228.

———; Fremouw, W. J.; and Reitz, A. L. 1982. A model useful in designing or describing evaluations of planned interventions in mental health. In *Practical program evaluation in youth treatment,* edited by A. J. McSweeny, W. J. Fremouw, and R. P. Hawkins, 24–48. Springfield, IL: Charles C. Thomas.

Mager, R., and Pipe, P. 1970. *Analyzing performance problems.* Belmont, CA: Fearon.

Meadowcroft, P.; Hawkins, R. P.; Trout, B. A.; Grealish, E. M.; and Stark, L. J. 1982. Making family-based treatment accountable: The issue of quality control. In *Behavioral treatment of youth in professional foster homes: An alternative,* chaired by E. L. Phillips. Symposium presented at the American Psychological Association Convention, Washington, DC.

Patton, M. 1979. *Utilization focused evaluation.* Beverly Hills, CA: Sage.

Peter, V. J. 1986. *What makes Boys Town so special.* Boys Town, NE: Father Flanagan's Boys' Home.

Peters, T. J., and Waterman, R. H. 1982. *In search of excellence: Lessons from America's best-run companies.* New York: Warner Books.

Phillips, E. L.; Baron, R. L.; Black D. D.; Coughlin D. D.; Fixsen, D. L.; and Maloney, D. M. 1981. *Advances in youth care.* 2nd ed. Boys Town, NE: Father Flanagan's Boys' Home.

———; Phillips, E. A.; Fixsen, D. L.; and Wolf, M. M. 1974. *The teaching family handbook.* Lawrence, KS: The University of Kansas Printing Service.

Quilitch, H. R. 1975. A comparison of three staff management procedures. *Journal of Applied Behavior Analysis* 8 (1): 59–66.

Reflections of current youth care paractices. 1979. Boys Town, NE: Father Flanagan's Boys' Home.

Reid, D. H., and Whitman, T. L. 1983. Behavioral staff management in institutions: A critical review of effectiveness and acceptability. *Analysis and Intervention in Development Disabilities* 3: 131–149.

Smart, D. A.; Smart, D. J.; Maloney, D. M.; Daly, P. B.; Daly, D. L.; and Fixsen, D. L. 1980. *Evaluation of an in-home consultation workshop.* Paper presented at the American Psychological Association Convention, Toronto.

Snodgrass, R. D., and Campbell, P. R. 1981. *Specialized Foster care: A community alternative to institutional placement.* Unpublished manuscript. Verona, VA. People Places, Inc.

Tavormina, J. B.; Hampson, R. B.; Grieger, R.; and Tedesco, J. 1977. Examining foster care: A viable solution for placement for handicapped children? *American Journal of Community Psychology* 5: 435–446.

Timbers, G. D.; Gross, N. F.; Judkins, B.; and Jones, R. J. 1982. Adaptation of the teaching-family model to specialized foster care. In *Youth Treatment in the "natural environment": The developing foster-family-based alternatives,* chaired by R. P. Hawkins. Symposium presented at the Association of Behavior Analysis Convention, Milwaukee, WI.

Vasaly, S. 1976. *Foster care in five states: A synthesis and analysis of studies from Arizona, California, Iowa, Massachusetts, and Vermont.* (BHEW Publication No. OHD 76-30097) Washinton, DC: George Washington University, Social Research Group.

Willner, A. G.; Braukmann, C. J.; Kirigin, K. A.; Fixsen, D. L.; Phillips, E. L.; and Wolf, M. M. 1977. The training and validation of youth preferred social behaviors of child care personnel. *Journal of Applied Behavior Analysis* 10: 219–230.

Ziarnik, J. P., and Bernstein, G. S. 1982. A critical examination of the effect of in-service training on staff performance. *Mental Retardation* 20 (3): 109–114.

Therapeutic Foster Care: Implications for Parental Involvement

ANTHONY N. MALUCCIO
JAMES K. WHITTAKER

T HE CRUCIAL SIGNIFICANCE OF biological parents for children in out-of-home placement has long been recognized. Studies have shown that parental involvement in the helping process and continuing parent-child contact are among the most prominent variables affecting the outcome of the placement as well as the child's development [Aldgate 1980; Fanshel 1975; Fanshel and Shinn 1978; and Rowe et al. 1984]. Parental involvement has therefore become a cornerstone of the recent movement to promote permanency planning for children and youth who are placed—or at risk of placement—out of their homes [Blumenthal and Weinberg 1984; Maluccio et al. 1986].

Particularly in light of its explicitly goal-oriented and treatment-focused nature, therapeutic foster care (TFC) provides many opportunities for effective parental involvement, along with varied challenges to the staff. This paper considers these opportunities and challenges and their implications for service delivery. Following a brief discussion of the rationale and purposes of involving biological parents, the focus is on implications and guidelines for promoting optimal parental involvement.

Background for Parental Involvement

There is an extensive rationale for maintaining parent-child contact and involving parents in treatment programs, even in situations in which the child must be permanently removed from the biological family.

Rationale

First, there is a strong philosophical base that speaks to the value of rearing children in a family setting. For instance, many writers emphasize that stability in living arrangements and continuity of relationships with parental figures promote a child's growth and development [e.g., Goldstein et al. 1973; Laird 1979].

Second, the importance of the family is supported by various theoretical perspectives, including the role of parent-child bonding in the development of human beings and the significance of the biological family in human connectedness and identity formation [Hess 1982; Laird 1979].

Third, there is evidence of the negative impact of separation on parents as well as children. Studies have shown that parents experience severe reactions such as depression [Jenkins and Norman 1972], while children exhibit symptoms of serious emotional disturbance [Bryce and Ehlert 1971].

Fourth, research shows that, when parents are not effectively involved, the gains that children make while in a foster family or a residential treatment program are often negated or reversed if they return to an unchanged home environment [Taylor and Alpert 1973]. And, finally, there are pragmatic reasons for involving parents; as Fanshel [1981: ix] has noted, biological "parents are by far the most likely source of permanency for children." In fact, a follow-up study of children discharged from foster care by a public children's services agency found that over two-thirds of the children were returned to their parents [Fein et al. 1983].

Impact of Permanency Planning Movement

Further support for parental involvement comes from the permanency planning movement that in recent years has been reshaping child welfare services [Blumenthal and Weinberg 1984; Maluccio and Fein

1983]. Permanency planning originally emerged as a response to the abuses of the child welfare system, especially the inappropriate removal of children from their homes and the recurring problem of "drift," or children being removed frequently from one out-of-home placement to another. As discussed elsewhere [e.g., Maluccio and Fein 1985; Maluccio et al. 1980; Maluccio et al. 1986], permanency planning was soon viewed as a vital means of dealing with the needs of children living away from their own families with little sense of stability or continuity in their living arrangements.

Permanency planning has been defined as:

> the systematic process of carrying out, within a brief time-limited period, a set of goal-directed activities designed to help children live in families that offer continuity of relationships with nurturing parents or caretakers and the opportunity to establish lifetime relationships. [Maluccio and Fein 1983: 197]

As reflected in this definition, permanency planning embodies a basic and nonrevolutionary idea: every child is entitled to live in a family, preferably his or her own biological family, in order to have the maximum opportunity for growth and development. It is an idea that has ancient origins, and it has been restated over and over throughout the history of child welfare [Shyne 1979]. Most recently, the goal of permanency for each child was embodied in federal legislation, the Adoption Assistance and Child Welfare Act of 1980 (Public Law 96–272), which mandates that states promote permanency planning for children coming to their attention, through such means as subsidized adoption; procedural reforms; and, above all, preventive and supportive services to families.

In essence, permanency planning refers to "the process of taking prompt, decisive action to maintain children in their own homes or place them permanently with other families" [Maluccio and Fein 1983: 195]. This does not mean that adoption, permanent foster care, or reunification of children with their families is inherently good or bad for everyone. It does mean that in each case there should be careful assessment and extensive work to maintain children with their own families, or to make other permanent plans when it has been demonstrated that the parents cannot care for the child. Through systematic and explicit attention to the role and involvement of biological parents,

TFC can become a prominent tool for implementing the provisions of P. L. 96–272 and achieving the goals of permanency planning.

Purposes of Parental Involvement

The effective involvement of biological parents in TFC programs requires careful analysis and assessment in each case. It is not something that should be undertaken casually. In all cases, however, the presumption should be that parents will be involved in one way or another, unless there are overwhelming contraindications, such as situations in which the parent's involvement can be demonstrated to be damaging to the child.

The degree and purposes of the involvement depend on a variety of factors, including the significance of the parents to the child; the motivation, qualities, capacities, and needs of parents and child; the reasons for placement; the developmental status of the child; and the nature of the permanency planning option being considered. Through analysis of these and other relevant factors, in collaboration with parents and children, an assessment is made regarding the degree, kind, and purpose of parental involvement.

Continuum of Parental Involvement

It is useful to think of parental involvement along a continuum, from minimum or nonexistent—as in cases in which termination of parental rights has been accomplished, or there is no viable family unit, or the youth is moving toward emancipation—to maximum, as in situations in which the plan is to reunify the child with his or her biological family. In most cases, the extent of parental involvement in the treatment program falls somewhere between these extremes; also, it may vary from time to time within the same case, with changes in the child's needs, parental motivation and behavior, family crises, treatment goals, and so forth. The key guideline should be that of encouraging maximum useful participation of parents in the program, including optimal contact with the child.

The process of analysis and assessment also serves to clarify the kind of parental involvement that should be promoted. For instance, should parent-child contact be in the own home, foster home, or agency setting? Should it be brief or extensive? Who should be present?

Should the interaction be structured and task-oriented or free-ranging? Should it be supervised? Should there be overnight visits? Should the parent be involved in decision making on behalf of the child, and if so, in which areas?

Specific Purposes

The extent and kind of parental involvement should of course be related to its primary functions, as agreed upon between clients and professionals, including such purposes as:

1. Reunification and integration of the child with the family of origin.

2. Providing a sense of continuity and family identity for the child. This purpose is increasingly seen as appropriate even in situations of adoption, particularly of older children, as exemplified in the growing practice of "open adoption."

3. Moving toward termination of parental rights, where necessary, and placement of the child in an alternate permanent plan, such as adoption.

4. Having parents help the child to separate from them and accept a new set of parents.

5. Helping parents and/or children to cope with the impact of separation and loss.

6. Providing the child with the opportunity to gain a realistic understanding of his or her parents and the family's problems.

7. Helping to resolve therapeutic issues, such as those involving resentment, guilt, or depression on the part of either parents or children.

8. Offering parents the opportunity to carry out their parenting roles, even in a limited way, and thus reducing their sense of failure and enhancing their sense of competence.

9. Helping to meet the parents' own needs, strengthen their coping skills and adaptive patterns, and deal more successfully with future life challenges.

10. Teaching the child and/or parents new interaction skills that will develop or maintain a more effective relationship.

By paying attention to these and other specific purposes of parental involvement and choosing the most appropriate ones on the basis of careful analysis in each situation, TFC programs can contribute not only to accomplishment of specific goals pertaining to the child, but also to the habilitation of parents and the prevention of further dysfunctioning in them and their families.

In our view, such a focus on parental involvement should be an *explicit, systematic* component of TFC. We would like to suggest various guidelines and implications for service delivery of such a component.

Viewing the Family as the Unit of Service

Focus on the Family

Promoting maximum parental involvement requires, first of all, that the family be regarded as the central unit of service or focus of attention, whenever possible and as much as possible. Human beings can best be understood and helped within their significant environment, and the family is the most intimate environment of all. It is here that the child develops and forms his or her identity and basic competence. The family has the potential for providing resources throughout the life cycle, especially as its members are sustained and supported by various services [Hartman and Laird 1983].

The family's own environment can be employed as the arena in which practitioners intervene to help strengthen communication, parenting skills, and parent-child relationships. It is for these reasons that researchers began intervening systematically in families in the 1960s [e.g., Hawkins et al. 1966; Tharp and Wetzel 1969; Wahler et al. 1965], and many appropriate programs and methods have been developed [e.g., Kinney et al. 1977; Kinney et al. 1981; Patterson et al. 1973; Wiltze and Patterson 1974].

The concept of the family as the central unit of attention, however, has often been difficult to implement in the human services, even though professionals have long concurred on its value. The tendency has been to fragment helping efforts by concentrating variously on the children, the parents, or the foster parents, rather than working with the children and parents as interacting components of one family system [Maluccio 1985]. Obstacles such as heavy caseloads, emergency situations, and complex family problems have often prevented us from fully incorporating into practice new knowledge about families and new approaches to intervention with family systems. Other factors, such as rescue fantasies and bias against parents, have complicated efforts to provide adequate services to families. In addition, there are obstacles such as the physical distance between the placement facility and the biological home and the reluctance of funding bodies to reimburse the agency for the cost of services to the parents.

While these obstacles are real, the evidence that family intervention is feasible and effective calls for an expansion of the concept and function of TFC, including commitment to the goals of permanency planning and the needs of parents; close interagency collaboration, particularly a public-private partnership; and designation of an appropriate staff member as the case manager to help plan, implement, and monitor services in behalf of the biological family.

Various authors have described programs and methods demonstrating what can be accomplished through a concentrated focus on the family [Alexander and Parsons 1973; Bryce and Lloyd 1981; Forehand and McMahon 1981; Hawkins et al. 1985; Horejsi et al. 1981; Kinney et al. 1977; Maluccio and Sinanoglu 1981; Maybanks and Bryce 1979; Sinanoglu and Maluccio 1981; Stein et al. 1978; Wiltze and Patterson 1974; Zeilberger et al. 1968]. These projects have shown that many parents can be rehabilitated and helped to plan responsibly for their children, through provision of comprehensive help involving both counseling and support services, emphasis on skill training, and systematic case management based on principles of decision making, goal setting, and contracting.

Even in situations in which children cannot be returned home, parents have been helped to participate in the planning process in a way that reflects their caring, helps maintain their dignity, and frees the child to move into another family [Jackson and Dunne 1981]. A common denominator in these programs is that parents are regarded as human beings with feelings and needs of their own, rather than being approached primarily in relation to what they may offer or mean to the child. The agency extends its responsibility to the parents in their own right. In addition, parents are helped to cope more decisively with their typical ambivalence toward their children.

In particular, the growth of the family therapy movement [e.g., Bowen 1978; Haley 1980; Minuchin and Fishman 1981] has led to the application of various family treatment approaches as alternatives to placement of children out of their homes or as methods of speeding up the reunification of placed children with their families.

Some agencies employ intensive, in-vivo family therapy with multiproblem families having children at risk of placement in substitute care [e.g., Kinney et al. 1977]. These programs stress the importance of viewing the family from an ecological perspective. Assessment and intervention focus on the family's transactions with its kinship system, school, community institutions, and other social networks. Intervention strategies are directed not only toward engaging the family in treatment but also toward changing the social systems that influence it [e.g., Tomlinson and Peters 1981].

Other agencies have gone even further in their work with families, experimenting with parent-child foster placements, in which single mothers and their abused or neglected children are placed jointly for time-limited periods in specialized foster homes. Along with affording immediate protection for the child, the placement facilitates assessment of the mother's functioning and the provision of intensive services to strengthen her parenting skills [Nayman and Witkin 1978].

Through similar approaches, TFC could take advantage of many opportunities for involving parents in the helping process and thereby helping both them and their children. In addition, there is the challenge of preserving family ties between children in alternate care and their families as much as possible. The natural bonds between children in care and their parents continue to be prominent for parents as well as children long after they are physically separated, reflecting the significance of the biological family in human connectedness and identity [Jenkins 1981; Laird 1979]. Practitioners should therefore regard the goal of preserving family ties as a major imperative of TFC. They should actively facilitate and support continued parent-child contact and interaction of the child with his or her total family unit.

Parental Visiting

A key means of accomplishing this preservation of family ties is consistent parental visiting of children in alternate care. As noted earlier, the findings of recent studies have highlighted the crucial role played by parent-child contact or parent visiting in the outcome of the placement as well as the child's functioning and development. For instance, research has demonstrated the importance of parental visiting of children in foster care as the best single predictor of the outcome of placement and, therefore, as the "key to discharge" [Fanshel 1975]. In their longitudinal study of foster care in New York City, Fanshel and Shinn [1978] found that children who were visited frequently by their parents during the first year of placement "were almost twice as likely to be discharged eventually as those not visited at all or only minimally" [p. 96]. Similarly, in a study conducted in Scotland, Aldgate [1980] reported that, in those cases where children had been returned to their families, "there had been some contact between at least one parent and child in 90% of the cases, and contact monthly or more frequently in just under half of the cases" [p. 29].

Of course, these are only correlations, and it may be that those children whose families seem most promising to professionals are the ones whose parents are encouraged most by professionals to be involved with the child. Experimental research would be needed to demonstrate convincingly that visiting plays a causal role in the outcome of the placement; but in the meantime we should assume that it plays at least some such role and proceed to assure visiting in most cases of children in out-of-home placement.

Studies have also found that high frequency of caseworker-parent contact is linked to a higher level of parental visiting [Fanshel and Shinn 1978] and to continued parental involvement with the child [Jenkins and Norman 1975]. There is, in addition, some evidence that visiting is correlated with the child's wellbeing and improved functioning while in care [Weinstein 1960]. In one study it was found that children who had been returned to their biological families from foster care did better in their ultimate permanent plans than those who had not had such a chance for parental connection [Fein et al. 1983]. Again, it is premature to conclude firmly that visiting or caseworker-parent contact are truly responsible for more favorable outcomes; but until firm evidence is available we should proceed on such assumptions.

In line with these findings, researchers have stressed the importance of encouraging and monitoring visiting: "agencies should be held accountable for efforts made to involve the parents in more responsible visitation" [Fanshel and Shinn 1978: 111]. The findings have also led to formulation of practice guidelines for using parent-child visiting as a means of achieving permanency planning [White 1981]. It has been stressed that "the visiting experience can be effectively used as a natural opportunity to provide services that meet the developmental needs of children and promote the competence of parents" [Sinanoglu and Maluccio 1981: 444].

Visiting also provides a significant opportunity to observe parent and child directly in interaction, and thus to assess their skills and relationship. The assessment and intervention functions can be enhanced if the professional, with the cooperation of the parent and youngster, arranges for simulation of various common problem situations [see McFall 1977]. These can first be used to assess parent and child behavior and then as a context for repeated and varied coaching by the professional, to build needed competencies.

As noted by Aldgate [1980], parent-child contact can enhance social functioning by assuring the child that he or she has not been rejected; helping the child and parents to understand why he or she cannot live at home; preventing the child's or parents' idealization of the parent; and helping parents maintain their relationship with their children. Others have also called attention to a neglected dimension: the significance of sibling relationships and the importance of maintaining sibling ties while children are in placement [Ward 1984]. All of these activities can influence the transactional sphere of the family and contribute to the goal of permanency planning in general, and the purposes of TFC in particular.

Contraindications

While we wish to underscore the value of preserving family ties and viewing the family as the unit of service, we also recognize that in some situations parental involvement is inappropriate. Although some parents will be sufficiently rehabilitated to be able to maintain, sustain, or resume care of their children, and others will accept their inability to do so and participate in making an alternate permanent plan, there are also parents who are not able to respond or who cannot be helped toward rehabilitation. In many of these cases, practitioners are compelled to ask: How can we manage to help the family overcome its difficulties within a time scale that does not damage the child? How far do we go in trying to help the parents? When is it time to give up? When should we move decisively to make another plan for the child?

As discussed elsewhere [Maluccio et al. 1986], there are certain factors that workers should consider in resolving these questions, although precise prescriptions are not available:

Age of child. In general, the younger the child, the more quickly a decision about a permanent plan needs to be made, to facilitate the child's bonding with parental figures.

Time. A parent's potential for rehabilitation "over time" is not enough. There must be an ability a rehabilitate within a "reasonable length of time," as determined on the basis of careful assessment of the child's needs, sense of time, and interests.

Previous efforts at rehabilitation. Where comprehensive and quality services have previously been provided for a sustained period with no indication of progress, the value of additional efforts should be questioned.

Chronicity of problems. When history reflects no time of stability for a family, and dysfunction has been a "way of life," there is less optimism about the potential for positive change. This is especially so when there is an established pattern of child abuse or neglect or an extensive history of incapacitating drug addiction.

Parents' investment. When parents are unwilling to participate in rehabilitative efforts, despite energetic, repeated, varied, and creative efforts to enlist their participation, an extended length of time is inappropriate.

In sum, in each case practitioners need to consider a variety of factors in making decisions about the extent and purpose of parental involvement, and about permanent plans for the child. Use of the service agreement or contract with parents [Stein and Rzepnicki 1983] can be an effective means of determining when sufficient efforts have been made or when the parents have gone as far as they can. Through active, therapeutic use of the service agreement, practitioners and parents can consider concretely when treatment goals have been accomplished, when there is reason to renegotiate new or additional goals, and when it is time to stop because the parents have demonstrated that they are unable to effect change or make use of the service.*

*Specific principles and techniques for working with parents who come to the attention of child welfare agencies are discussed in Blumenthal and Weinberg 1984; Horejsi et al. 1981; Kaplan 1986; Maluccio et al. 1986; and Stein and Rzepnicki 1983.

Restructuring the Family's Environment

It is a major function of the service delivery system in child welfare to help families of children in care to restructure their environment, to modify or enrich it so that it is more suited to their needs and more conducive to their positive functioning [Maluccio 1981a]. TFC programs cannot be expected to play such a role totally; but they should be actively involved in it, in conjunction with other community agencies or systems working with the child and his or her family.

Methods of Restructuring the Environment

A major means of restructuring the environment and helping the family is a creative partnership between professional helpers and social support networks [Whittaker and Garbarino 1983]. Professionals can help parents to identify actual or potential resources in their social networks, such as neighbors, friends, members of the kinship system, or other informal helpers. The extended family may provide resources to help parents care for a child so as to avert placement in an unfamiliar institution or foster home, or reduce the duration of the placement.

In other cases, restructuring the environment may mean involving parents in a self-help group or introducing a new person such as a homemaker or parent aide. Various studies have shown the value of complementing professional help with the services of paraprofessionals such as home management specialists, homemakers, and older persons who model effective parental behavior and coping skills [Miller et al. 1984; Spinelli and Barton 1980]. These aides help to meet the basic needs of parents, enrich the family's environment, and prevent placement or replacement. They provide parents with better opportunities to learn or relearn skills, fulfill needs, and develop competence. The introduction of a new, supportive person such as a grandparent figure helps meet the needs of parents themselves and enhances their capacity to give to their children.

Comprehensive Services

In response to the multiple needs of families in basic life areas, many programs stress the provision of intensive services and environmental supports to the child's family before placement, during placement, and in the aftercare period. These comprehensive programs seek to avoid placement or reduce its duration and reunite children with their own families by strengthening the parents' coping and adaptive capacities and providing them with necessary services, including counseling. Some examples are described in Jones et al. [1976], Kinney et al. [1977], Sherman et al. [1973], and Weissman [1978].

A major feature of these programs is collaboration among various community resources. Especially noteworthy is the approach of the Lower East Side Family Union in New York City to avert or limit foster care; it involves careful coordination and monitoring of services provided to families at risk by a variety of agencies [Weissman 1978]. This approach takes into account the complex personal and environmental factors that affect family functioning and structure, and is also sensitive to the needs, qualities, and values of minority group families and children, who are overrepresented in foster care [Olsen 1982; Shyne and Schroeder 1978].

Adopting a Competence Perspective

Effective parental involvement can also be facilitated by having practitioners adopt a competence perspective or growth orientation in their work with parents of children in placement. They should stress approaches that serve to empower their clients—parents or children— to enhance their competence in dealing with environmental challenges [Maluccio 1981b]. Knowledge from ego psychology, behavioral psychology, biology, ecology, and other fields can guide practitioners in engaging the progressive forces within clients and helping them to develop their competence. For example, behavior modification has stressed competence-building, as with the "constructional approach" described by Schwartz and Goldiamond [1975], and the competency-based casework model delineated by Gambrill [1983].

Deemphasis of Pathology

Pathology should be deemphasized, especially psychopathology [Schwartz and Goldiamond 1975], and greater emphasis placed on clients as active, striving human beings. At present, there is a tendency to view the problems leading to foster care of children as reflecting primarily the psychopathology of the parents. There is inadequate attention to societal conditions that limit the power of parents and interfere with their coping efforts.

Minuchin [1970], among others, has urged that social agencies shift from a pathological model to an ecological approach, in order to be more effective in their work with the poor. He points out that social interventions deriving from the pathological model have tended to fragment families; in contrast, regarding the family as part of an eco-system can elicit and use the supportive resources in the environment and help hold it together. Minuchin concludes that the adoption of an ecological perspective could lead to more "truly change-producing and helpful" interventions in support of families and their children, poor or otherwise [p. 130].

In particular, "human problems, needs, and conflicts need to be translated into adaptive tasks providing the client with opportunities for growth, mastery, and competence development" [Maluccio 1979: 290], and emphasis should be placed on the resources and supports needed by parents. For example, a parent who is labeled abusive or neglectful can be helped to learn or relearn skills in child care. To accomplish this, the problem has to be redefined as a situation involving lack of knowledge or inadequate parenting skills. In short, the focus is on identifying and removing obstacles that interfere with the parents' coping capacities and on providing growth-producing supports.

Parents as Resources

In addition, adopting a competence perspective means regarding parents as resources in their own behalf—as partners in the helping process—rather than simply as carriers of pathology, as is often the case. As we shift from a pathological view of parents to a competence orientation, we are better able to identify strengths in parents themselves and involve them in growth-producing activities. As they are given adequate opportunities, parents and other family members can mobilize their own potentialities and natural adaptive strivings.

Self-Help Groups

As demonstrated in recent years by the success of various self-help groups such as Parents Anonymous, parents can be recognized as resources who can help each other. Practitioners should aim toward empowering clients to accomplish their purposes and meet their needs through individual and collective efforts, as Solomon [1976] has argued in her book on empowerment in black communities. For parents of children in foster care, working together to obtain needed resources for a better life for themselves and their children is an excellent way to counteract powerlessness and promote competence and self-esteem [Carbino 1981].

Self-help groups have proven effective with parents from varied socioeconomic and ethnic backgrounds. For example, Leon et al. [1984] describe a self-help group for Hispanic mothers, who benefited in a number of ways: building personal relationships and mutual support systems with others sharing similar concerns and interests; feeling free to express their problems and anxieties as parents; strengthening their self-esteem and increasing their self-confidence in parenting; and learning how to negotiate the various service delivery systems.

Parent Training

In addition to paving the way for parents to participate in groups pertinent to their needs, practitioners can help them become involved in parent training programs. Parents of children in TFC usually need help with parenting; they need to learn or relearn skills to enhance their functioning as parents. Through such help, they are more likely to be able to care for their children permanently. In many agencies, parent training is offered to foster parents regularly [Hampson 1985; Stone and Hunzeker 1974]; yet biological parents need training even more urgently, and greater efforts should be made to provide it.

Opportunities for parent training may be offered directly by the agency or treatment center. Others are available through community resources such as schools, family service agencies, child welfare agencies, and self-help organizations [Abidin 1980; Turner 1980]. Practitioners generally find that most biological parents can make use of these resources, in conjunction with counseling services or other treatment programs [Turner 1980].

As with any professional intervention, it is important to assess with the parents what is needed. For instance, do the parents recognize any needs in relation to their parenting? What are the areas in which they need to build or improve skills in child care? What is the parents' competence in areas such as interactional skills, behavior management, and the stimulation of cognitive development? Participation in parent training programs geared to the needs and qualities of parents can enhance their competence and lead to more constructive involvement with their children.

Redefining the Roles of Parents and Practitioners

Therapeutic foster care programs also need to redefine the roles of professionals working directly with biological parents, as well as the roles of foster parents and biological parents themselves.

Professional Roles

Practitioners often are understandably overwhelmed by the complex and intense demands placed on them as they seek to work with parents. A major problem is that they are, in a sense, asked to be all things to all people: therapists for child and parents; consultants or supervisors with foster parents; case managers; advocates; and so on. Moreover, these multiple roles are frequently carried out in the context of insufficient training, heavy caseloads, inadequate supervision, and limited resources.

For optimal parental involvement, the major role of the key practitioner or case manager working with the parents should be redefined as that of a catalyst or enabling agent, someone who actively and systematically helps the family to identify or create and use necessary resources. The worker uses flexible approaches and calls on a variety of resources to help provide the conditions necessary for parents to achieve their purposes, meet life's challenges, and engage in their developmental processes. Above all, rather than relying primarily on traditional psychotherapeutic techniques such as insight-oriented procedures, practitioners should become experts in methods of environmental modification, use of existing community resources and natural helping networks, creation of new resources that may be needed by their clients, and mobilization of family members' own resources. As a catalyst, for example, the case manager or key practitioner may link parents and children with other professionals providing direct services such as teaching of skills.

Roles of Biological and Foster Parents

The relationship between biological parents and foster parents, or other substitute caretakers such as child care staff members, needs to be redefined; in contrast to the traditional pattern of keeping them apart or in competition with each other, efforts should be made to have parents, foster parents, and other child care personnel regard themselves as partners in a shared undertaking, with common goals and mutually supportive and complementary roles.

Such a perspective could lead to new helping systems that are ultimately more effective and rewarding for everyone concerned. For example, several articles describe the involvement of foster parents as resources for parents through such means as role modeling or serving as parent aides [Davies and Bland 1978; Ryan et al. 1981]. As suggested in these articles, foster parents can become allies of biological parents and be more actively involved in the treatment plan in behalf of each family, as long as their roles are clarified and they are provided with adequate supports and rewards. In other words, ways should be found in at least some cases to enable a foster family to become an extension of the biological family, rather than its substitute, as is now the case [Watson 1982]. The foster family could become an integral part of the overall treatment program and help promote the adaptive functioning of the biological parents.

Conclusion

Therapeutic foster care offers the challenge of optimal involvement of parents and a substantial contribution to permanency planning. Such a challenge presents agencies and practitioners with varied opportunities to work with parents as an integral feature of treatment.

To exploit these opportunities in behalf of children and their families, we must go beyond implicitly or explicitly regarding biological parents as unmotivated, untreatable, unresponsive, or hard-to-reach. We must show total commitment to parental involvement with children in out-of-home placement.

In the face of diminishing resources and increasing demands for services, such a perspective on parental involvement may seem overly ambitious or idealistic. Yet, although the world's physical resources are limited, human resources are underutilized; and the resources of biological parents remain largely untapped. Through active parental participation, we can help parents to mobilize their resources and become partners in permanency planning for their children.

REFERENCES

Abidin, R. R., ed. 1980. *Parent education and intervention handbook.* Springfield, IL: Charles C. Thomas.

Aldgate, J. 1980. Identification of factors influencing children's length of stay in care. In *New developments in foster care and adoption,* edited by J. Triseliotis, 22–40. London: Routledge and Kegan Paul.

Alexander, J. F., and Parsons, B. V. 1973. Short-term behavioral interventions with delinquent families: Impact on family process and recidivism. *Journal of Abnormal Psychology* 81: 219–225.

Blumenthal, K., and Weinberg, A., eds. 1984. *Establishing parent involvement in foster care agencies.* New York: Child Welfare League of America.

Bowen, M. 1978. *Family therapy in clinical practice.* New York: Aronson.

Bryce, M., and Ehlert, C. 1971. 144 Foster children. *Child Welfare* 50: 499–503.

———, and Lloyd, C., eds. 1981. *Treating families in the home—an alternative to placement.* Springfield, IL: Charles C. Thomas.

Carbino, R. 1981. Developing a parent organization: New roles for parents of children in substitute care. In *The challenge of partnership: Working with parents of children in foster care,* edited by A. N. Maluccio and P. A. Sinanoglu, 165–186. New York: Child Welfare League of America.

Davies, L., and Bland, D. 1978. The use of foster parents as role models for parents. *Child Welfare* 57: 380–386.

Fanshel, D. 1975. Parental visiting of children in foster care: Key to discharge? *Social Service Review* 49: 493–514.

———. 1981. Foreword. In *The challenge of partnership: Working with parents of children in foster care,* edited by A. N. Maluccio and P. A. Sinanoglu, ix–xi. New York: Child Welfare League of America.

———, and Shinn, E. B. 1978. *Children in foster care—a longitudinal investigation.* New York: Columbia University Press.

Fein, E.; Maluccio, A. N.; Hamilton, V. J.; and Ward, D. 1983. After foster care: Outcomes of permanency planning for children. *Child Welfare* 62: 485–562.

Forehand, R. L., and McMahon, R. J. 1981. *Helping the noncompliant child: A clinician's guide to parent training.* New York: Guilford.

Gambrill, E. 1983. *Casework: A competency-based approach.* Englewood, NJ: Prentice-Hall.

Goldstein, J.; Freud, A.; and Solnit, A. 1973. *Beyond the best interests of the child.* New York: The Free Press.

Haley, J. 1980. *Leaving home.* New York: McGraw-Hill Book Company.

Hampson, R. 1985. Foster parent training: Assessing its role in upgrading foster home care. In *Foster care: Current issues, policies, and practices,* edited by M. J. Cox and R. D. Cox, 167–205. Norwood, NJ: Ablex Publishing Corp.

Hartman, A., and Laird, J. 1983. *Family-centered social work practice.* New York: The Free Press.

Hawkins, R. P.; Meadowcroft, P.; Trout, B. A.; and Luster, W. C. 1985. Foster family-based treatment. *Journal of Clinical Child Psychology* 14: 220–228.

———; Peterson, R. F.; Schweid, E.; and Bijou, S. W. 1966. Behavior therapy in the home: Amelioration of problem parent-child relations with the parent in a therapeutic role. *Journal of Experimental Child Psychology* 4: 99–107.

Hess, P. 1982. Parent-child attachment concept: Crucial to permanency planning. *Social Casework* 63: 46–53.

Horejsi, C. R.; Bertsche, A. V.; and Clark, F. W. 1981. *Social work practice with parents of children in foster care: A handbook.* Springfield, IL: Charles C. Thomas.

Jackson , A. D., and Dunne, M. J. 1981. Permanency planning in foster care with the ambivalent parent. In *The Challenge of partnership: Working with parents of children in foster care,* edited by A. N. Maluccio and P. A. Sinanoglu, 151–164. New York: Child Welfare League of America.

Jenkins, S. 1981. The tie that binds. In *The challenge of partnership: Working with parents of children in foster care,* edited by A. N. Maluccio and P. A. Sinanoglu, 151–164. New York: Child Welfare League of America.

———, and Norman, E. 1972. *Filial deprivation and foster care.* New York: Columbia University Press.

———, and ———. 1975. *Beyond placement: Mothers view foster care.* New York: Columbia University Press.

Jones, M. A.; Neuman, R.; and Shyne, A. 1976. *A second chance for families.* New York: Child Welfare League of America.

Kaplan, L. 1986. *Working with multiproblem families.* Lexington, MA: Lexington Books, D. C. Heath.

Kinney, J.; Madsen, B.; Fleming, T.; and Haapala, D. A. (1977). Homebuilders: Keeping families together. *Journal of Consulting and Clinical Psychology* 45: 667–673.

———; Haapala, M. A.; and Gast, E. J. 1981. Assessment of families in crisis.

In *Treating families in the home,* edited by M. Bryce and J. C. Lloyd, 50–67. Springfield, IL: Charles C. Thomas.

Laird, J. 1979. An ecological approach to child welfare: Issues of family identity and continuity. In *Social work practice: People and environments,* edited by C. B. Germain, 174–209. New York: Columbia University Press.

Leon, A. M.; Mazur, R.; Montalvo, E.; and Rodriguez, M. 1984. Self-help support groups for Hispanic mothers. *Child Welfare* 63: 261–268.

Maluccio, A. N. 1979. Promoting competence through life experiences. In *Social work practice: People and environments,* edited by C. B. Germain, 282–302. New York: Columbia University Press.

———. 1981a. An ecological perspective on practice with parents of children in foster care. In *The challenge of partnership: Working with parents of children in foster care,* edited by A. N. Maluccio and P. A. Sinanoglu, 22–35. New York: Child Welfare League of America.

———, 1981b. *Promoting competence, a new/old approach to social work practice.* New York: The Free Press.

———. 1985. Biological families and foster care: Initiatives and obstables. In *Foster care: Current issues, policies, and practices,* edited by M. A. Cox and R. D. Cox, 147–166. Norwood, NJ: Ablex Publishing Corp.

———; Fein, E.; Hamilton, J.; Klier, J.; and Ward, D. 1980. Beyond permanency planning. *Child Welfare* 59: 515–530.

———, and ———. 1983. Permanency planning: A redefinition. *Child Welfare* 62: 195–201.

———, and ———. 1985. Permanency planning revisited. In *Foster care: Current issues, policies and practices,* edited by M. J. Cox and R. D. Cox, 113–133. Norwood, NJ: Ablex Publishing Corp.

———; ———; and Olmstead, K. A. 1986. *Permanency planning for children: Concepts and methods.* London and New York: Tavistock Publications and Methuen, Inc.

———, and Sinanoglu, P. A., eds. 1981. *The challenge of partnership: Working with parents of children in foster care.* New York: Child Welfare League of America.

Maybanks, S., and Bryce, M., eds. 1979. *Home-based services for children and families.* Springfield, IL: Charles C. Thomas.

McFall, R. M. 1977. Analogue methods in behavioral assessment. In *Behavioral assessment: New directions in clinical psychology,* edited by J. Check, D. Cone, and R. P. Hawkins, 152–177. New York: Brunner/Mazel.

Miller, K.; Fein, E.; Howe, G. W.; Gaudio, C. P.; and Bishop, G. V. 1984. Time-limited, goal-focused parent aide service. *Social Casework* 65: 472–477.

Minuchin, S. 1970. The plight of the poverty stricken family in the United States. *Child Welfare* 59: 124–130.

———, and Fishman, H. C. 1981. *Family therapy techniques.* Cambridge, MA: Harvard University Press.

Nayman, L., and Witkin, S. L. 1978. Parent/child foster placement: An alternative approach in child abuse and neglect. *Child Welfare* 57: 249–258.

Olsen, L. 1982. Services for minority children in out-of-home care. *Social Services Review* 56: 572–585.

Patterson, G. R.; Cobb, J. A.; and Ray, R. S. 1973. A social engineering technology for retraining the families of aggressive boys. In *Issues and trends in behavior therapy,* edited by H. E. Adams and I. P. Unikel. Springfield, IL: Charles C. Thomas.

Rowe, J.; Cain, H.; Hundleby, M.; and Keane, A. 1984. *Long-term foster care.* London: Batsford Academic and Educational.

Ryan, P.; McFadden, E. J.; and Warren, B. L. 1981. Foster families: A resource for helping parents. In *The challenge of partnership: Working with parents of children in foster care,* edited by A. N. Maluccio and P. A. Sinanoglu, 189–199. New York: Child Welfare League of America.

Schwartz, A., and Goldiamond, I. 1975. *Social casework: A behavioral approach.* New York: Columbia University Press.

Sherman, E. A.; Neuman, R.; and Shyne, A. W. 1973. *Children adrift in foster care.* New York: Child Welfare League of America.

Shyne, A. W., ed. 1979. *Child welfare perspectives—selected papers of Joseph H. Reid.* New York: Child Welfare League of America.

———, and Schroeder, A. G. 1978. *National study of social services to children and their families.* DHEW Publication NO. OHDS-78-30150. Washington, DC: U. S. Government Printing Office.

Sinanoglu, P. A., and Maluccio, A. N., eds. 1981. *Parents of children in placement: Perspectives and programs.* New York: Child Welfare League of America.

Solomon, B. 1976. *Black empowerment: Social work in oppressed communities.* New York: Columbia University Press.

Spinelli, L. A., and Barton, K. S. 1980. Home management services for families with disturbed children. *Child Welfare* 59: 43–52.

Stein, T. J.; Gambrill, E. D.; and Wiltse, K. T. 1978. *Children in foster homes: Achieving continuity of care.* New York: Praeger.

———, and Rzepnicki, T. L. 1983. *Decision making at child welfare intake.* New York: Child Welfare League of America.

Stone, H. D., and Hunzeker, J. M. 1974. *Education for foster family care: Models and methods for foster parents and social workers.* New York: Child Welfare League of America.

Taylor, D. A., and Alpert, S. 1973. *Continuity and support following residential treatment.* New York: Child Welfare League of America.

Tharp, R. G., and Wetzel, R. J. 1969. *Behavior modification in the natural environment.* New York: Academic Press.

Tomlinson, R., and Peters, P. 1981. An alternative to placing children: Intensive and extensive therapy with "disengaged" families. *Child Welfare* 60: 95–104.

Turner, C. 1980. Resources for helping in parenting. *Child Welfare* 59: 179–187.

Wahler, R. G.; Winkel, G. H.; Peterson, R. F.; and Morrison, D. C. 1965. Mothers as behavior therapists for their own children. *Behavioral Research and Therapy* 3: 113–124.

Ward, M. 1984. Sibling ties in foster care. *Child Welfare* 63: 321–332.

Watson, K. W. 1982. A bold, new model for foster family care. *Public Welfare* 40: 14–21.

Weinstein, E. 1960. *The self-image of the foster child.* New York: Russell Sage Foundation.

Weissman, H. H. 1978. *Integrating services for troubled families.* San Francisco, CA: Jossey-Bass.

White, M. S. 1981. Promoting parent-child visiting in foster care: Continuing involvement within a permanency planning framework. In *Parents of children in placement: Perspectives and programs,* edited by P. A. Sinanoglu and A. N. Maluccio. New York: Child Welfare League of America.

Whittaker, J. K., and Garbarino, J. 1981. *Social support networks: Informal helping in the human services.* New York: Aldine Publishing Company.

Wiltze, N. A., and Patterson, G. R. 1974. An evaluation of parent training procedures designed to alter inappropriate aggressive behavior of boys. *Behavior Therapy* 5: 215–221.

Zeilberger, J.; Sampen, S. W.; and Sloane, H. N., Jr. 1968. Modification of a child's problem behaviors in the home with the mother as therapist. *Journal of Applied Behavioral Analysis* 1: 47–53.

IV

Future Directions for Therapeutic Foster Care

Introduction to
Part 4

PREDICTING THE FUTURE IS always risky, but the past few years have seen such an increase in the number of therapeutic foster care (TFC) programs—as suggested by the increase from 48 returned questionnaires in the 1984 survey conducted by Bryant and Snodgrass (reported in this volume) and 157 returned (and qualifying) questionnaires in the 1987 survey conducted by Nutter et al. (1988)—that it seems reasonable to predict that TFC will continue to be developed in more and more corners of North America and, perhaps, the world. Although most TFC programs appear to have developed largely independent of other TFC programs, this is less than ideal. Each such independently-developed program is likely to be constrained by traditions and attitudes of traditional foster family care, because that will be the most obvious model nearby, and each such program will be denied much of the benefit of what others conducting TFC have learned.

An alternative is to first study (preferably in person) available model programs and available evidence of their success with the kind of youngsters and families one hopes to serve, then hire consultants from that program to assist in developing the new program. In this way, the new program stands on the shoulders of the original model program and can then go on to develop and evaluate further improvements on that model. Several states and localities have recently followed this strategy, using People Places [Bryant 1980; Bryant et al. 1986],

PRYDE [Hawkins et al. 1985], or perhaps another program as a model.

Even when a model is adopted, there still remains the question—for both those in the model program and those adopting the model—whether it is best to replicate the model with very high fidelity or to adapt it. High-fidelity replication requires more effort on the part of both the personnel coming from the model and those adopting the model; because, if they are serious about fidelity they will check for it carefully and directly, and they will need documentation of various processes by the staff [cf. Hawkins et al. 1982]. The first chapter in this section, by William Davidson and colleagues, presents briefly the results of some difficult research evaluating whether high-fidelity replication or "reinvention" (local adaptation) is a better approach. They also review current knowledge about the dissemination of programs in criminal justice and education, both of which are fields closely related to TFC, and they apply this knowledge to TFC.

Not only does the Davidson et al. analysis suggest that high-fidelity replication is better than modifying the prototype (except when the modification is adding components), the authors also raise questions as to whether any TFC models have been sufficiently evaluated to serve as a model, discuss the evidence of effectiveness that a potential adopter should require, point out the risk of developing TFC that is only nominally different from regular foster family care, and point to the need to evaluate replicate sites as well as the original model.

In the second chapter of this section, Robert Friedman argues that our future efforts should achieve not just a range of child mental health and care services, or even a continuum of services, but a planned, integrated system of services for children. He describes the role of TFC in such a system.

He raises vital questions for those of us who are proudly conducting TFC programs and acclaiming their value—questions that may provoke greater humility and partially redirect our efforts. These questions have to do with whether youngsters and their environments are being assessed adequately before TFC placement is decided, and with the need for comparative evaluation of TFC and other program types [e.g., De Fries et al. 1970; Hawkins et al. 1988]. He points out that TFC is not the least restrictive intervention, and that at least one program of intensive home-based intervention directly in the child's family home has proven both effective and cost effective [Kinney et al. 1977].

Friedman encourages us to develop intensive home-based intervention programs or components alongside or within our TFC programs, routing promising children and their families into the former instead of, or prior to, placement in the latter. Of course, given the limited success obtained by any mode of treatment with chronically antisocial youngsters such as those that some TFC programs serve [cf. Wolf et al. 1987; Hawkins and Meadowcroft 1984], it is unlikely that more than a small fraction of the clientele in such programs could have been diverted by home-based intervention; but most programs probably have at least some youngsters who could be served adequately through such intervention.

Friedman also urges us to collect and provide client-descriptive and program-descriptive data on our programs, so that some kinds of meaningful evaluation of outcomes is possible (cf. Hawkins et al. 1982]. Finally, he advises us as to what we can expect in the way of resistance or receptiveness to TFC and its dissemination.

REFERENCES

Bryant, B. 1980. *Special foster care: A history and rationale.* Verona, VA: People Places, Inc.

———; Snodgrass, R. D.; Houff, J. K.; Kidd, J.; and Campbell, P. 1986. *The parenting skills training.* Staunton, VA: People Places, Inc.

De Fries, C.; Jenkins, S.; and Williams, E. C. 1970. Foster family care for disturbed children: A nonsentimental view. In *Child welfare services: A sourcebook,* edited by A. Kadushin, 193–209. London: MacMillan.

Hawkins, R. P.; Almeida, M. C.; Samet, M.; and Conaway, R. 1988. *The effectiveness of behavioral foster-family-based treatment compared with other placements of disturbed/disturbing youth.* Poster presented at the Association for Advancement of Behavior Therapy, New York.

———; Meadowcroft, P.; Trout, B. A.; and Luster, W. C. 1985. Foster family-based treatment. *Journal of Clinical Child Psychology* 14: 220–228.

———; Fremouw, W. J.; and Reitz, A. L. 1982. A model useful in designing or describing evaluations of planned interventions in mental health. In *Practical program evaluation in youth treatment,* edited by A. J. McSweeney, W.

J. Fremouw, and R. P. Hawkins, 24–48. Springfield, IL: Charles C. Thomas.

Nutter, B.; Hudson, J.; and Gallaway, B. 1988. *A survey of specialized foster care in North America.* Paper presented at the Second North American Conference on Treatment Foster Care, Calgary, Alberta.

Wolf, M. M.; Braukmann, C. J.; and Ramp, K. A. 1987. Serious delinquent behavior as part of a significantly handicapping condition: Cures and supportive environments. *Journal of Applied Behavior Analysis* 20: 347–359.

The Dissemination of Therapeutic Foster Care: Implications from the Research Literature

WILLIAM S. DAVIDSON II
JEFFREY P. MAYER
RAND GOTTSCHALK
NEAL SCHMITT
CRAIG H. BLAKELY
JAMES G. EMSHOFF
DAVID ROITMAN

THE COINCIDENCE OF THE development of therapeutic foster care (TFC) and the demand for fiscal accountability has created a situation in which a mid-range alternative between regular foster family care and institutionalization is needed. Given the growth of TFC, the demands for dissemination of successful models will be intense. Our original interest in the field of dissemination research was due to frustration with our own unsuccessful attempts to disseminate innovative social programs [Rappaport et al. 1977]. This paper focuses on the implications of that research on the dissemination of eight social programs in criminal justice and education. The research was funded by the National Science Foundation [Blakely et al. 1984].

Little scientifically valid information is available about the dissemination of social programs. Sarason [1977] indicated a decade ago that we know a good deal about how organizations function, but we know little or nothing about how they are initiated or disseminated. That observation still rings largely true today.

This paper first reviews briefly the current knowledge concerning dissemination of social programs: an overview of the literature and a brief report of the author's own pertinent research. We then discuss applying current knowledge about the dissemination of social programs to TFC from both the point of view of the disseminator and the potential adopter.

Overview of the Research Literature

The development and dissemination of social programs has been conceptualized according to theories originally developed to explain the spread of agricultural, medical, and engineering innovations. The research, development, and diffusion model (R, D, & D) is an important conceptual base that underpins most technology transfer and planful dissemination operations. This model of programmatic change has been described as a series of stages. First, a new program or process (the innovative social technology) is developed and piloted, with careful attention to evaluating its impacts and outcomes. This step in the process is usually characterized by program design, initial operation, and careful data collection and evaluation. This step, one hopes, also involves research aimed at identifying the components of the prototype program that produce the observed effects. In this way, superstitious and nonessential program components can be eliminated and replication of effects maximized. Second, if efficiency and effectiveness are demonstrated, the prototype program is made available to potential adopting organizations. Once adopted, it is assumed that the effects that were observed in the prototype will be replicated by the adopting unit and its clients [Fairweather and Tornatzky 1977; Guba 1968].

In the classical R, D, & D model, it was assumed that users and adopters considered evaluation results to be very important in their decisions to adopt and use new programs and procedures. It was further assumed that implementation of the innovation proceeded nearly automatically once the decision to adopt had been made. This is essentially the "better mousetrap" model of social program improvement, which included the assumption that when a program is adopted, as when a mousetrap is purchased, the whole thing is acquired intact, in good working order. Several pieces of research have indicated, however, that intact implementation is not automatic. The way in which an innovation is implemented differs across organizations and settings. The process of implementation is influenced by the type of innovation being disseminated [Berman and McLaughlin 1978; Eveland et al. 1977; Farrar et al. 1979; Fullan and Pomfret 1977; House et al. 1972]. It is also the case that adopters of prototype social programs typically have a local adjustment in mind when the decision to start a new program is made.

The results of several studies produced considerable rethinking of the conceptual basis of dissemination efforts. Havelock [1969] and others proposed a "linkage" model that was a modified version of the original R, D, & D position. This linkage model is similar to the formal training in the Teaching Family model. Instead of treating adopters of the Teaching Family model as passive observers, they were recruited actively. Implementation was not considered automatic; instead, systematic training, consultation, and technical assistance were provided to the Teaching Family homes. Four important components in this modified R, D, & D model are: (1) the importance of maintaining the fidelity of the replication; (2) the effectiveness of the replication, given the criteria on which the pilot program was developed; (3) the adaptation or reinvention of the pilot program during local implementation; and (4) the continuing operation or routinization of the program. Since these four concepts provide a framework within which the existing literature can be understood and a framework for discussion of implications of dissemination research for TFC specifically, the next section highlights these four variables.

Some Key Concepts in Dissemination

Fidelity and effectiveness. As alluded to above, fidelity concerns the similarity of a replication innovation, as implemented, to the original innovation that was to be disseminated. That is, fidelity is the extent to which an adopting agency or setting implements a program that closely resembles the original prototype. A minor war has been fought in the published literature over whether or not high fidelity replications are desirable. Those advocating high fidelity conceptualize social innovations as consisting of a number of well-specified or at least specifiable components. These advocates argue that rigorously developed and evaluated programs should be so implemented that they very closely resemble the original prototype program [Boruch and Gomez 1977; Calsyn et al. 1977; Hall and Loucks 1978; Sechrest and Redner 1978; Datta 1981]. Another school of thought on the matter can be labeled "proadaptation." Researchers and practitioners advocating an adaptation position argue that differing organizational and community contexts and practitioner needs demand on-site modification of virtually all social programs [Berman and McLaughlin 1978; House et al. 1972]. Thus, an important issue in the dissemination of social programs is the proposed relationship or lack thereof, between program fidelity and program effectiveness. The extent to which there is a strong relationship between the presence of particular program components and ultimate effectiveness determines the defensibility of the profidelity stance.

Stated in contemporary political terms, this debate is also between strategies of local versus centralized control of social programs. On the one hand, the profidelity camp, consistent with a centralized control point of view, argues that a strong relationship exists between specific program components and program effectiveness. Hence it is critical that there be close correspondence between the prototypic procedures and local program operation. For adopters of new social programs, this means that it is necessary to receive considerable training and consultation from the prototype developers while any new social program is being implemented.

On the other hand, the proadaptation camp minimizes the importance of one-to-one correspondence between prototypic programs and subsequent replicates. While still maintaining the importance of the major themes and goals of the original prototype, the local-control viewpoint emphasizes the desirability of a local version of the program. Within this model, it is highly desirable that adopters of prototypic programs adapt them to local needs, philosophies, personnel, and settings.

Reinvention.   Sometimes adaptation is referred to as reinvention. This term was introduced by Rogers and his colleagues to capture the flavor of an active process of change in the implementation of an innovative social program by adopters [Eveland et al. 1977; Rice and Rogers 1979]. Reinvention may bring to mind the phrase "not invented here," a slogan that has been used to reject the ideas of outsiders simply because they originated elsewhere. But that is not the connotation intended here. Instead, the connotation here is that the program is reinvented locally to allow a crucial sense of program ownership, which affects enthusiasm and commitment.

It is important to distinguish between lack-of-fidelity and reinvention; otherwise, the notion of reinvention has no independent utility to researchers or practitioners. At least two alternative defintions of reinvention are possible, each of which would distinguish reinvention from lack-of-fidelity [Blakely et al. 1984]. One type of reinvention is the addition of a program component to an existing prototype, a component that in no way interfered with the operation of the original program components. This could include, for example, the provision of a service to an additional clientele or the application of procedures to a new domain. A second type of reinvention would be the procedural modification of one of the prototype's components without changing (or at least diminishing) its original function, its effects. This could include changing the setting in which a program component was used, or the replacement of a program component with a highly related but not identical procedure. This second type of modification would be exemplified by a teacher using a more recent set of math curriculum materials similar to those used in the prototypic classroom's curriculum.

Routinization.   Routinization is another aspect of program dissemination. It is the degree to which the innovation becomes part of the normal practice of an organization. Similar concepts are institutionalization [Berman and McLaughlin 1978] and durability [Glaser and Backer 1977; 1980]. In general, research focused on routinization has attempted to describe the processes and determinants by which social programs become standard operating procedure. Describing the correlates of social program routinization has led to an examination of the determinants of program longevity. In fact, a good deal of early research on routinization used longevity as the operational definition of routinization. The influential work of Yin [1978], however, suggested that routinization should be broken into two component parts: full incorporation and longevity.

Yin has carried out the most extensive work on routinization. In his original study, he examined the routinization of six technological innovations in 19 urban bureaucracies. Using a retrospective design, he concluded that routinization could be conceived of as the survival of the program through ten passages and cycles. It was suggested that the survival of an innovative program was achieved by passing through particular critical events in the history of an organization, such as moving from soft to hard money, surviving the departure of key personnel, the establishment of formal job descriptions, and the disappearance of being perceived as special or new.

Yin found that routinization was more than the age of an innovation. In other words, program longevity and durability were not consistently related to program incorporation, that is, to movement through his hypothesized passages and cycles. Further, for different organizational contexts and for different innovations, different periods of time would be needed to achieve any given passage and cycle.

It has commonly been the case that routinization is confused with program effectiveness. All too often, program longevity, incorporation, routinization, and survival are substituted for systematic examinations of effectiveness. For the new program developer, the goal is to spawn more adoptions that survive. For the new program adopter, routinization is seeing the new special project become part of the usual functioning of the host agency or its context.

Relationships between reinvention and routinization.   The relationship between reinvention and routinization has also received some attention from researchers. Glaser and Backer [1977] argued that local adaptation of innovative programs would promote routinization to the extent that local adaptation countered the not-invented-here reaction, and to the extent that adaptation provided implementers with a sense of ownership and investment in the program. For example, Berman and McLaughlin [1978] discovered that teacher participation in decision making enhanced routinization through a similar sense-of-ownership mechanism. The sense-of-ownership hypothesis suggests that highly reinvented innovations will tend to be highly routinized.

In another study, Glaser and Backer [1980] compared several innovations that were terminated within two years with four that had survived for more than two years. They found that those programs that survived had experienced substantial reinvention and had high levels of staff support and involvement in decision making; and, further, that they had successfully closed organizational performance gaps.

A Multi-Innovation Investigation of Dissemination Dimensions

Given the critical nature of the issues already outlined, a study was designed to examine more systematically the relationship between fidelity, reinvention, effectiveness, and routinization [Emshoff et al. 1980]. The relevance of this research for the dissemination of TFC homes stems from two characteristics of the research: (1) it involved an examination of the complete innovation life cycle instead of focusing only on innovation adoption [Tornatzky and Klein 1982]; and (2) it included multiple innovations within multiple organizations, as contrasted with the case study of only one or two innovations or organizations. Both of these characteristics are critical since TFC is not dissimilar to some of the innovations examined, and certainly TFC programs can take place within many multiple organizational contexts.

It is well beyond the scope or intent of this chapter to report the findings of our research in detail, but a brief summary follows. The interested reader is invited to request a copy of the full study from the authors or is referred to Blakely et al. [1984].

Overview of Methodology

To select innovations for investigation, criteria were established that (1) guaranteed a reasonable number of replicates for each of eight programs to be studied; (2) demanded that innovations be organization-wide in nature (to avoid inclusion of individual implementation); and (3) required two years of operation (to allow time for full-scale implementation). These procedures resulted in the selection of the eight innovations described in figure 1.

Ten organizations that had adopted and were using each of these innovations were sampled for site visits. In other words, there were ten organizations per innovation or a total of 80 organizations (sites) in the sample. One primary focus of this study was the systematic observation and measurement of program fidelity, program effectiveness, program reinvention, and program routinization. For each of these variables, measurement procedures were developed.

In measuring program fidelity, the measurement model of Hall and Loucks [1978] was employed. This began with interviewing the original program developers and conducting content analyses of writ-

Education

Help One Student to Succeed (HOSTS)—A diagnostic, prescriptive, tutorial reading program for children in grades 2–6. Tutors are community volunteers and high school students. The program includes "pulling out" students from their regular classes at least one-half hour per day.

ECOS Training Institute (ECOS)—A training program to help principals and teachers infuse new content areas into existing curricula or add new content areas. A major part is the formation of a committee composed of administrators, teachers, and students. Deals with all grade levels.

Experience-Based Career Education (EBCE)—This program provides experience outside of school at volunteer field sites for the student. Systematic career and interest exploration on the part of the student is also encouraged. The development of an individualized learning plan for each student is carried out. Program concerns high school students.

Focus Dissemination Project (FOCUS)—A "school within a school" for disaffected junior and senior high school students. All students are required to participate in a group of 8–10 students and one leader (called Family). Students take at least one class in the Focus program. Classes in the Focus program involve individualized, self-paced instruction.

Criminal Justice

One Day/One Trial (ODOT)— A jury management system that calls in a certain number of potential jurors per day. Potential jurors come in for that day and if not selected to serve in a trial, have completed their obligation.

Community Arbitration Project (CAP)—Juvenile offenders are sent to a formal arbitration hearing run by the court intake division, rather than to courts. Juveniles have the specific consequences of their actions explained to them. Youths are then given a number of hours of informal supervision usually involving work in the community.

Community Crime Prevention (SCCPP)—This program is a three-phase attack on residential burglary. This involves the setting up of a neighborhood block watch, property marking and inventory, and home security inspections.

Pre-Release Center (MCPRC)—Involves the setting up of a residential facility separate from the prison. This facility should be in the community from which most of the inmates are drawn. Inmates are encouraged to work so that they will have a job when they are released. Counseling and social awareness instruction is also part of this program.

Figure 1
Innovations Selected in the Present Study

ten materials, resulting in specification of program components that were observable, logically discrete, innovation specific, and exhaustively descriptive of the innovation. On the basis of systematic observation, each component was rated as existing at an "ideal," "acceptable," or "unacceptable" level. A rating of ideal was given when the replicated program component matched the prototype in all respects. A rating of acceptable was given when there were some minor differences between the replicated component and the prototype that did not appear to change the function, frequency, or intensity of the component. A rating of unacceptable reflected a difference between the replicated component and the prototype that did appear to change the function, frequency, or intensity of the component. Research teams spent two full days at each site collecting data. Interrater agreement for fidelity was 81%.

Each of the eight innovations being investigated had been evaluated before dissemination. The same outcome criteria used in the original evaluations were used as the measure of effectiveness for this study. Since there was wide variability in the amount and quality of effectiveness data across sites, a rank-ordering procedure was employed. Relative effectiveness was determined for each replication site by having two pairs of researchers independently rank sites within each innovation program, resulting in two sets of rankings. The correlation across raters for ranked effectiveness was .90.

To assess reinvention, research team members took note of any activity, procedure, material, or facility that did not fit within the framework of the innovation components and/or their variations. Extensive notes were taken during and immediately following site visits. These were then coded into instances of reinvention that involved additions, and instances that involved modifications, and each was rated as to the degree of departure from the original model. Interrater agreement on both types of data averaged 80%.

Routinization was measured in terms of incorporation (the degree to which an innovation becomes standard practice) and longevity (actual and expected length of use). Ratings of incorporation by research team members were accomplished using Yin's [1978] concepts of programs surviving critical passages and cycles. The incorporation measure had an interrater agreement rate of 93%. Expected longevity ratings were taken directly from program staff members during on-site interviews. A reliability coefficient of .82 was obtained for the longevity items.

Brief Description of Results

Three sets of results are pertinent to our discussion here. First, what was the degree of program fidelity observed? In other words, what can reasonably be expected in terms of replicating complex social programs like TFC, given systematic efforts at promoting fidelity in such replication? The results from our research indicated that all eight innovations had acceptable overall fidelity scores; that is, the mean fidelity score of components in each program fell in the acceptable range. This would indicate that a good deal of fidelity can be expected if care is taken in promoting adherence to prototypic models.

The second research question involved the degree of routinization of these eight programs across their ten replication sites. Overall, these programs demonstrated a moderate degree of routinization. Nearly three-quarters of the innovations were in an expansion phase in their life cycle, suggesting a moderate degree of routinization. Most respondents felt that their programs would continue.

The third issue, and the one most critical here, is the observed relationship between fidelity, effectiveness, incorporation, expected longevity, and total reinvention in the replication sites. Positive and statistically significant relationships existed between fidelity and effectiveness, fidelity and reinvention, and reinvention and effectiveness. Thus, it appeared that fidelity and reinvention were not contradictory but were occurring simultaneously. Furthermore, the higher-fidelity, higher-reinvented programs tended also to be more effective.

At first, these results seemed to both support and contradict a profidelity position. However, given that reinvention was defined unusually, by including both additions and modifications, it was possible for a replication to rate high in reinvention while also rating high in fidelity. Additional partial correlations were conducted to assess whether fidelity or reinvention had the greater association with program effectiveness.

The partial correlation between fidelity and effectiveness, holding reinvention constant, was positive and significant, on the one hand. On the other, the partial correlation between reinvention and effectiveness, holding fidelity constant, indicated no relationship at all. Thus, fidelity seems to have made the more important contribution to program effectiveness.

Further, the two forms of reinvention—addition and modification—were analyzed separately. This analysis showed that additive reinvention was related to greater program effectiveness, while modification of prototype components was not significantly related to effectiveness. In addition, by using partial correlation techniques that held modification constant, the study again found a significant positive relationship between addition and effectiveness. Similar analysis with modifications failed to uncover any relationship, suggesting that modifying components of a proven prototype generally does not improve its effectiveness.

Surprisingly, none of the relationships between the two measures of routinization and other variables were significant. Of particular interest were the relationships between reinvention and routinization. "Sense-of-ownership" and "commitment" hypotheses would suggest a strong positive relationship between reinvention and routinization, but the results from this study did not reveal any such relationships.

Further, there were no significant relationships between incorporation and expected longevity, supporting Yin's contention that program age was not directly tied to a program's moving through the various phases of routinization.

Another important finding was that there was only a moderate, nonsignificant, positive association between routinization and effectiveness. This is a particularly important finding in light of the common assumption—in the dissemination and model-adoption literature, and among human service professionals in general—that effectiveness will lead to program longevity and incorporation [Glaser and Backer 1980].

Implications for TFC

We turn now to the implications of these findings and issues for the dissemination of TFC models. Viewing them as new social programs that will be disseminated, it is important to use current knowledge about dissemination. As noted earlier, the knowledge base concerning the dissemination process is meager, considering the complexity of the practical tasks involved in the spread of social programs. Given what we do know, however, we can delineate a series of educated guesses about how to proceed with the dissemination of TFC.

Expected Demand

Social programs commonly spread as a result of variables other than demonstrated effectiveness, as the research reported here and in the literature indicates [Blakely et al. 1984; Fairweather et al. 1977]. This holds at least two implications for TFC. First, it should be recognized that the current interest in TFC is largely for reasons other than actual effectiveness. Strong programmatic, fiscal, legal, and ideological demands for new models of residential child care, as mentioned earlier, have encouraged the development of TFC.

A second implication of the research affects both developers and potential adopters of TFC programs. The pressure for new programs will lead to the temptation to adopt programs and procedures that are popular and have shown their ability to survive, not programs that have been proven effective. One of the clear implications of existing knowledge about dissemination processes is that potential adopters of social programs should demand effectiveness data from developers, particularly data that go well beyond the opinion or testimonial of the prototype program's director and staff.

A third implication of the research has to do with the fidelity of each TFC program to a prototype. Assuming that the prototype is effective, the research suggests that increasing the fidelity of TFC programs to the prototype on which they are based would be likely to produce comparable levels of effectiveness in these replicate programs; altering or eliminating components of the prototype will not likely contribute to either effectiveness or longevity. This implies that potential adopters of TFC procedures should demand, from the prototype site, both extensive procedure manuals and ongoing technical support for program implementation and operation. Social programs of the complexity of TFC cannot be totally reduced to manuals and formal training sessions, though both are quite important. Social programs are more than words, they involve specific actions, roles, and procedures that need careful tuning in the face of particular situational demands.

Issues Raised by Current Knowledge

The research to date also points out the importance of viewing TFC as a total social program. Although it is possible to construe TFC as a particular set of home management techniques, the work of Hall and Loucks [1978] and Blakely et al. [1984] suggests that social programs are more accurately viewed as organizational entities. Hence issues of foster parent recruitment, agency requirements, and so forth, are all critical components of TFC. A broad conceptualization of TFC that includes such variables should, in turn, enhance the specification of each particular program model. To the extent that the specification then enhances fidelity in both the original site and the replication sites, it should also maximize effectiveness. Additionally, construing models of TFC broadly may encourage the type of program addition (as an important subset of reinvention possibilities) related to ultimate effectiveness.

The current state of knowledge concerning the dissemination process also provides some important warnings for TFC models. A good deal of previous research on the dissemination process has pointed out the difficulty of maintaining innovations that require genuine role change [Fairweather et al. 1974; Rappaport et al. 1977]. TFC models appear to require real role change on the part of foster parents and staff members, and changes in methods of financial support, compared to the human services to which TFC is most closely related: foster care, residential child care, mental health, and corrections. At issue is the extent of manifest versus true adoption of TFC. Merely changing the labels for activities in foster homes will do little to change their effectiveness.

Both developers and adopters should be aware that obtaining and maintaining high fidelity implementation and operation of planned TFC procedures may actually be impeded by the use of previous foster parents or adults who have had their own children, both of whom are accustomed to particular roles in relation to children. Some specific models of TFC require adhering to particular principles of child rearing; yet philosophies about child rearing remain one of the last bastions of rugged individualism in this country. Hence, a large number of potential foster parents have had previous roles, learning histories, and ideologies relevant to interacting with children, and these may be at odds with the specific procedures used in any particular TFC model. The need for careful monitoring of implementation and dissemination efforts is thus magnified.

It is also important to note the changes that are required of organizational arrangements and supports with TFC. For example, most TFC models require far closer interaction between the support staff, such as caseworkers, and the foster parents than is available or prevalent in most public child placement agencies—a sharp change, indeed.

Given the complexity of TFC and the state of research to date, adopters of TFC programs should not assume that identical results will be produced in a replication site. Too many community, personnel, and other variables of unknown impact are involved. Therefore, continuing evaluation of TFC program replicates is crucial. This research should include examination of the particular conditions under which the components of TFC programs are effective or produce inconsistent outcomes.

Conclusion

It seems inevitable that the demand for TFC programs will support their widespread dissemination before the accumulation of adequate, detailed scientific knowledge of the dissemination process or even the effectiveness of the prototype programs. The forces supporting dissemination are strong and timely. What our current knowledge about dissemination can provide at the moment are some guideposts concerning important processes. We know that social programs can be complex and that processes to ensure implementation fidelity, evaluation of effectiveness, reinvention only where needed, routinization, and continued evaluation are important. Perhaps most important is the need for additional research. The dissemination of TFC provides an excellent opportunity for experimental and exploratory research. The frequency with which new programs are disseminated in the child care field requires that we move quickly to enhance our understanding of these critical events.

REFERENCES

Berman, P., and McLaughlin, M. W. 1978. *Federal programs supporting educational change: Implementing and sustaining innovations.* Santa Monica, CA: Rand Corporation.

Blakely, C.; Roitman, D.; Gottschalk, R.; Mayer, J.; Schmitt, N.; Davidson, W. S.; and Emshoff, J. G. 1984. *Salient processes in the dissemination of social technologies.* Final report to the National Science Foundation, Grant No. ISI-7920576. East Lansing, MI: Michigan State University, Department of Psychology.

Boruch, R. F., and Gomez, H. 1977. Sensitivity, bias, and theory in impact evaluation. *Professional Psychology* 8: 411–433.

Calsyn, R.; Tornatzky, L. G.; and Dittmar, S. 1977. Incomplete adoption of an innovation: The case of goal attainment scaling. *Evaluation* 4: 128–130.

Datta, L. E. 1981. Damn the experts and full speed ahead: An examination of the study of federal programs supporting educational change as evidence against directed development for local problem-solving. *Evaluation Review* 5: 5–32.

Emshoff, J. G.; Davidson, W. S.; and Schmitt, N. 1980. *Salient processes in the dissemination of social technology* (Research grant submitted to the National Science Foundation.) East Lansing, MI: Michigan State University.

Eveland, J. D.; Rogers, E.; and Klepper, C. 1977. *Innovation process in public organizations: Some elements of a preliminary model.* Springfield, VA: NTIS.

Fairweather, G. W., and Tornatzky, L. G. 1977. *Experimental methods for social policy research.* New York: Pergamon.

Farrar, E.; deSanctis, J. E.; and Cohen, D. K. 1979. *Views from below: Implementation research in education.* Cambridge, MA: Huron Institute.

Fullen, M., and Pomfret, A. 1977. Research on curriculum and instruction implementation. *Review of Educational Research* 47: 335–397.

Glaser, T., and Backer, T. 1977. Innovation redefined: Durability and local adaptation. *Evaluation* 4: 131–135.

———, and ———. 1980. Durability of innovations: How goal attainment scaling programs faired over time. *Community Mental Health Journal* 16: 130–143.

Guba, E. G. 1968. Diffusion of innovations. *Educational Leadership* 25: 292–295.

Hall, G. E., and Loucks, S. F. 1978. *Innovation configurations: Analyzing the adaptation of innovations.* Paper presented at the annual meeting of the American Educational Research Association, Los Angeles, CA.

Havelock, R. G. 1969. *Planning for innovation through dissemination and utilization of knowledge.* Ann Arbor, MI: Institute of Social Research.

House, E. R.; Kerins, T.; and Steele, J. M. 1972. A test of the research and development model of change. *Educational Administration Quarterly* 8: 1–14.

Rappaport, J.; Seidman, E.; and Davidson, W. S. 1977. Demonstration research and manifest versus true adoption: The natural history of a research project to divert adolescents from the legal system. In *Social and psychological research in community settings,* edited by R. F. Munoz, and L. R. Snowden, 101–131. San Francisco, CA: Jossey-Bass.

Rice, R. E., and Rogers, E. M. 1979. Reinvention in the innovation process. *Knowledge: Creation, Diffusion, Utilization* 1: 499–514.

Sarason, S. B. 1977. *Work, aging, and social change.* New York: The Free Press.

Sechrest, L. B., and Redner, R. 1978. Strength and integrity of treatments. In *Review of criminal evaluation results.* Washington, DC: National Criminal Justice Reference Service, U.S. Department of Justice.

Tornatzky, L. G., and Klein, K. J. 1982. *Innovation characteristics and innovation adoption-implementation: A meta-analysis of existing findings.* Washington, DC: National Science Foundation.

Yin, R. 1978. *Changing urban bureaucracies: How new practices become routinized.* Santa Monica, CA: The Rand Corporation.

The Role of Therapeutic Foster Care in an Overall System of Care: Issues in Service Delivery and Program Evaluation

ROBERT M. FRIEDMAN

T HE GROWTH IN THERAPEUTIC foster care (TFC) described in this volume represents an important development for efforts to strengthen services for children and adolescents with special needs, and particularly those with emotional problems. This paper describes recent developments in services for emotionally disturbed children, places TFC programs within this context, and discusses some of the issues these programs should deal with as they grow further.

System of Care

The Joint Commission on the Mental Health of Children [1969], after studying children's mental health services in the United States, concluded that services were woefully lacking, and that there was a critical need to develop a range of services for children and their families and to bring various child-serving agencies into more cooperative working relationships. Up to this point, the services in communities were for clinic-based outpatient services and little else, except for relatively restrictive, sometimes damaging residential or hospital place-ment. If a child and family could not be served adequately in outpatient treatment, typically for one-hour per week, then the next step, because it was the only step available, was often an expensive and restrictive residential placement.

Unfortunately, the status of services in many communities has not changed dramatically since that time [Knitzer 1982; United States Office of Technology Assessment 1986]. From a conceptual and tech-nical standpoint, however, considerable progress has been made and is now contributing to changes in services in many communities.

Initially, the efforts to improve services in the 1970s focused on adding specific services that were intended to have major effects in and of themselves. These included such programs as day treatment and group homes. For example, among proponents of behavioral ap-proaches there was a particular enthusiasm for group homes, as de-veloped under the Teaching Family model [Kirigin et al. 1982; Phillips 1968], and for parent training models [Patterson 1974; O'Dell 1974].

In the late 1970s and 1980s the focus changed, with an increased emphasis on a range of services—sometimes called a continuum of care, and sometimes called a system of care [Behar 1986; Knitzer 1982; United States Office of Technology Assessment 1986; Stroul and Friedman 1986]. The basic rationale for a system of care with a broad range of services is that it offers maximum flexibility to provide the specific services that an individual and his or her family require and only those services. Without a well-planned range of services, there are few options to choose from. The concept of a system of care not only recognizes the differences between different individuals at any single point in time but also takes into account the expectation that the needs of a particular child and family will change over time and over treat-ment.

The concept of treatment flexibility is therefore the fundamental underpinning for such a system. A strong emphasis is also placed on family-focused and community-based treatment, and treatment in the least restrictive environment appropriate to a child's needs [Stroul and Friedman 1986].

As pointed out by Hawkins et al. [1982], the concept of restric-tiveness should not be confused with the concept of treatment intensity. In fact, one of the major developments of the last ten to 15 years in children's mental health has been the recognition that very intensive services—in terms of the number of hours of active intervention—can be provided within family settings, and do not require hospital settings. Although children may spend more actual hours in a hospital setting per day than they do in other treatment settings, the hospital may actually provide less intensive treatment than other services unless these hours are used for active treatment.

There is no single model of a system of care that is universally accepted. However, the model presented by Stroul and Friedman [1986], developed as part of the Child and Adolescent Service System Program of the National Institute of Mental Health, has broad acceptance. As illustrated in figure 1, this model emphasizes preventive services, nonresidential services, and residential services. It includes both crisis and noncrisis services. Included as part of the overall model is a description of services within related systems and a strong emphasis on a set of "operational services," such as case management [see Update 1987 for a discussion of case management services].

Role of Therapeutic Foster Care in a System of Care

Within this system model, TFC is presented as the least restrictive of the residential alternatives. This is not to suggest, however, that it is less intensive than the other models, or less well equipped to serve children with severe problems (e.g., Meadowcroft and Almeida 1987). In fact, several recent reviews have concluded that there is no evidence to indicate that the more restrictive residential models described in figure 1—therapeutic group care, residential treatment centers, wilderness camps, or inpatient hospitals—are either more intensive or more effective than less restrictive services such as day treatment, intensive family-based services and TFC [Friedman and Street 1985a; Gutstein 1987; Lowman 1987; United States Office of Technology Assessment 1986].

Indeed, if there has been any consistent finding in the research literature on the effectiveness of residential care, as limited and imperfect as that research has been, it has been the finding reported in this volume by Whittaker and Maluccio that "success in residential care, however defined, is largely a function of the supports available in the posttreatment community environment and has much less to do with either the presenting problem or the type of treatment offered." Partly because of the importance of the postdischarge environment, Curry [1986] emphasizes that residential treatment should be considered just one step of an ongoing treatment process that begins before placement

Figure 1—COMPONENTS OF THE SYSTEM OF CARE

1. *Mental Health Services*
   Prevention
   Early Identification & Intervention
   Assessment
   Outpatient Treatment
   Home-Based Services
   Day Treatment
   Emergency Services
   Therapeutic Foster Care
   Therapeutic Group Care
   Therapeutic Camp Services
   Independent Living Services
   Residential Treatment Services
   Crisis Residential Services
   Inpatient Hospitalization

2. *Social Services*
   Protective Services
   Financial Assistance
   Home Aid Services
   Respite Care
   Shelter Services
   Foster Care
   Adoption

3. *Educational Services*
   Assessment & Planning
   Resource Rooms
   Self-Contained Special Education
   Special Schools
   Home-Bound Instruction
   Residential Schools
   Alternative Programs

4. *Health Services*
   Health Education & Prevention
   Screening & Assessment
   Primary Care
   Acute Care
   Long-Term Care

5. *Vocational Services*
   Career Education
   Vocational Assessment
   Job Survival Skills Training
   Vocational Skills Training
   Work Experiences
   Job Finding, Placement &
      Retention Services
   Sheltered Employment

6. *Recreational Services*
   Relationships with Significant
      Others
   After School Programs
   Summer Camps
   Special Recreational Projects

7. *Operational Services*
   Case Mangement
   Self-Help & Support Groups
   Advocacy
   Transportation
   Legal Services
   Volunteer Programs

From Stroul and Friedman, 1986.

and continues after discharge, rather than being viewed as the treatment itself.

While there is no evidence to support the view that more restrictive residential placements are more intensive or effective than TFC, similarly there is no evidence to suggest that TFC is more effective than some of the intensive nonresidential services, such as intensive home-based services and day treatment, which are generally even less restrictive. The most frequently utilized intensive home-based service model comes from the work of the Homebuilders project in Tacoma, Washington [Kinney et al. 1977]. Within this approach, trained crisis counselors, with caseloads of about two to four families at a time, may work with a particular family for as many as 20 hours per week. The intervention is time-limited (usually four to six weeks), but the intensity is such that a variety of "hard" and "soft" services can be provided.

Friedman and Street [1985a] review the effectiveness of this approach and conclude that families for whom removal of a member seemed imminent can often be kept together and improve in function, and that this has revolutionized the concept of "in need of out-of-home placement." One recent study has demonstrated greater effectiveness of an intensive nonresidential intervention such as this in contrast to residential care, at least in the short run [Auclaire and Schwartz 1987].

The fields of day treatment and case management have not been as dominated by a single treatment model as has intensive home-based intervention. However, the evaluations that have been conducted of these services indicate that they have considerable potential for effectively serving difficult and multiproblem clients [see Update 1986a and 1987 for reviews].

What are the implications of these findings, and of these program innovations for TFC? For one thing, they suggest that, given the apparent power of intensive nonresidential approaches, TFC programs need to demonstrate that the youngsters they are serving do, in fact, need to be out of their home, and could not be served using even less restrictive approaches. The demonstration may be relatively easy in instances where youngsters have already been out of their home for many years before entering a TFC program. A demonstration is more difficult, however, and more crucial for youngsters who are being removed from their biological family specifically to enter a TFC program. For such youngsters we need to ask whether they have had an opportunity to be served in the most intensive of the nonresidential services before being removed from their own home.

If this question is not asked, and if there is not careful documentation of services previously received, then demonstrations of effective treatment by TFC programs will appropriately be subject to question. Did these children need to be removed from their homes? Could they not have been served as effectively and less expensively in nonresidential services? Would not such nonresidential services have been more consistent with values that emphasize preserving the integrity of families if at all possible?

Within many communities, the types of intensive nonresidential services briefly described here may not be available. In such instances, from a clinical standpoint, the treatment of children in TFC programs is clearly justified. From a systems perspective, however, and from an evaluation perspective, it becomes problematic to determine if in fact the placement was needed, or was simply an available alternative.

Evaluation Challenge

As the children's services field progresses to a more sophisticated and planned system of care, on the one hand, and to a more value-oriented approach that emphasizes treatment within a family context and in the least restrictive environment, on the other hand, the evaluation challenge for a particular treatment service will become more complex. The task will become one of demonstrating not only that the treatment offered is viable and produces particular changes in children and their families, but also that the changes could not have taken place at less cost, and at less disruption to the child and family.

To date, TFC programs have largely focused on the challenge of demonstrating that they are a viable alternative to more restrictive and costly residential placements, such as in inpatient hospital settings or residential treatment centers. There is a tremendous need in the field for such alternatives, and although studies directly comparing different residential treatment models are rare, the initial evidence is at least tentatively encouraging for TFC [Update 1986b].

This encouraging finding is exciting and much needed, and TFC programs are to be commended for their early efforts at evaluation. At the same time, however, they are to be reminded of the need for more and better studies. And these studies must not only compare TFC with other residential programs, but also compare it with less restrictive interventions.

The challenge to examine TFC in relation to less restrictive, non-residential services is a compelling one that must not be overlooked, for several reasons. First, from a values standpoint, a philosophical standpoint, and a legal standpoint, there continues to be an emphasis on family-focused treatment, and treatment in the least restrictive setting. Public Law 94–142, the Education for All Handicapped Children Act, emphasizes this, for example, as does Public Law 96–272, the Adoption Assistance and Child Welfare Act. Within P.L. 96–272, the requirement is imposed that reasonable efforts be made to keep a family intact before a child is removed. The specific definition of "reasonable efforts" remains vague, but some states are moving to operationalize this definition. For example, in Illinois, legislation was pased in 1987 providing "family preservation services" [Edna McConnell Clark Foundation 1985]—basically another term for intensive home-based services such as in the Homebuilders model—as an "entitlement" for families before a child is removed. Given this strong value and legal base, combined with the encouraging findings on the efficacy of intensive home-based interventions and the absence of adequate funds for human services in most states, there is likely to be an increased focus on maintaining children in their own home if at all possible.

Second, as already indicated, the research literature on the effectiveness of residential treatment suggests the importance of aftercare services and the posttreatment environment [Friedman and Street 1985b; Whittaker and Maluccio, this volume]. This issue has not been adequately discussed in the literature on TFC, and few programs have presented descriptions of follow-through services that they provide, or any data on long-term outcomes [an exception is the PRYDE program, Hawkins et al. 1985]. Given the consistent finding that the postdischarge environment is important, resistance will probably increase to expending large sums of money on out-of-home placements rather than on strengthening the family environment. TFC programs need to be aware of this both in their efforts to work within communities, and in their program and clinical efforts with individual children and their families. Indeed the family should be involved throughout the entire time a child is in treatment, regardless of the setting [see Maluccio and Whittaker, this volume].

Third, the most innovative and exciting developments in the children's services field are in such areas as intensive home-based services, day treatment, case management (particularly when it includes individualized service planning with wraparound services), individualized treatment approaches in general, crisis work, and TFC. Restrictive residential settings are viewed in the public sector more and more as an unfortunate necessity for some youngsters, but not as a cause for optimism. In the public sector, the wave of the future is clearly with intensive and individualized services that are flexibly funded and less restrictive than inpatient hospital settings and residential treatment settings. This is not the case in the private for-profit sector, but the trends there appear to be more fueled by the profitability of hospitals and residential treatment centers—due to the availability of third-party payments—rather than to the demonstrated need for or effectiveness of these services [Gutstein 1987; Lowman 1987].

Considering this trend in the public sector, and the improved technologies of the last years, there is an important need for TFC programs to be evaluated as part of an overall system of care in which the nonresidential services are made increasingly more effective and important. It will no longer be sufficient for TFC programs to demonstrate their effectiveness only in relation to more restrictive residential care, given the existing doubt about the effectiveness of such residential placements and the promising developments in nonresidential services.

Fourth, in the early stages of the development of TFC programs many youngsters have been referred from more restrictive residential settings. If TFC programs are successful in demonstrating that they are a viable alternative to such restrictive programs to begin with, then the percentage of their referrals from such programs will diminish. Referrals of children still living with at least one relative or in a regular foster home will correspondingly increase. Under such circumstances, it is especially important to demonstrate that TFC in fact, as a more restrictive placement, is necessary.

Future Directions

Given this set of circumstances, there are several additional recommendations to be offered concerning future efforts to determine both the effectiveness of TFC and its role within a community-based system of care. The first recommendation builds upon the actual services provided by TFC programs, while the others are more strictly research oriented.

Several individuals have noted that although there is no single model of TFC, there are a number of features that are common to such programs [Snodgrass and Bryant, this volume; Stroul and Friedman 1986; Webb 1988]. These features include intensive work with each child and family, individualized programming for the youngsters, training and other support for the treatment parents, small caseloads for the program staff members, and a capacity to make an immediate response in times of crisis. To a large extent, these are much the same features that are embodied in the Homebuilders approach to intensive home-based services; within this model, workers are continuously available, they not only provide counseling but also general support and assistance with other family needs, workers have small caseloads, and treatment programming is individualized [Edna McConnell Clark Foundation 1985]. Importantly, neither type of service is quick to give up on children or families, or likely to be discouraged by the particular diagnostic label that a child or parent has, or the child's service history. In fact, providers of intensive home-based services and TFC are likely to feel very much at home with each other's approach.

Given this compatibility of approach, one strategy of service development that may enhance overall effectiveness of treatment for children and families and at the same time strengthen program evaluation efforts would be for agencies to provide both types of services. Under such a model, children and families with severe problems and at the verge of having a child removed would be referred to the agency. The initial response of the agency would be to work intensively with the family in an effort not only to stabilize the crisis situation but to use it to enhance family functioning. If at any point, however, the agency decided that a child was in significant danger by remaining in the home, or that it was otherwise in the child's best interest to be removed, then the services of the TFC program could be rapidly accessed.

This approach would in a sense use the intensive home-based services as the gatekeeping mechanism for youngsters to leave their own home (or a regular foster home), when necessary, to enter TFC. It would enhance services in the community and support the objectives of providing family-focused treatment and maintaining as many children in their own homes as possible. The role of the TFC services would remain critical, but having the intensive home-based service in addition would assure that youngsters referred from a less restrictive option to TFC would not be placed in it unless truly requiring the service.

This is a strategy that calls for agencies to diversify their services. Given the multiple needs of youngsters and families, and the need to promote continuity of care, diversification would be advantageous for community referral agents. A broadening of services would be manageable for provider agencies, too, since intensive home-based services and TFC embody similar procedures of treatment. One example of a program that has successfully achieved such a diversification is the Youth

Residential Services of Summit County, Ohio. This agency began with a residential treatment program, added a TFC model [Gedeon 1986], and has now developed an intensive home-based treatment component.

One implication of this approach for TFC programs should be made explicit: under such a model, the program may find that it is serving a more difficult clientele than before. For example, a well-conducted intensive home-based intervention program may succeed in maintaining a large percentage of the youngsters it serves in their families. For purposes of illustration, suppose that this is accomplished with 60% of the youngsters served. The TFC program would then be left to deal with the 40% that present the most difficult situations. One impact of this would be to reduce the success rate (however that is measured) of the TFC program from perhaps 70% to 50%.

A reduction in apparent success is deceptive, however. If the program can demonstrate that it is now serving more difficult youngsters—perhaps in terms of the descriptive characteristics of the youngsters and the previous services they received—then it may in fact be providing a greater community service with the lower success rate than it was previously with the higher success rate. Its role within a community-based system of care may be clearer as well.

This may be of little consolation to agency staff members if funding agencies identify the apparent decrease in the success rate as a problem. But if the provider plans jointly with the funding source for the diversification, and they agree on the advantages of it, then the risks can be minimized.

Related to this need to document the severity of the youngsters' problems, it should be pointed out that one of the weak links of all program and systems evaluation in children's services is the inadequacy of the description of the youngsters and families served. Good description is often absent, even simple demographic information, and objective or standard instruments are often not used. This makes it impossible to determine the comparability of youngsters in different programs, and to evaluate adequately the effectiveness of programs [Hawkins et al. 1982].

As TFC programs grow, one recommendation is that they consider a voluntary effort to collect at least some comparable data on their client population to facilitate comparison both between different TFC programs, and between such programs and other components of a system of care. Such an effort was begun for a number of programs in Florida [Friedman 1983] but has been discontinued now.

Considering the rapid pace of growth of TFC programs, and the increased support being evidenced for them, there will be a tendency for more and more groups to call their services by the same name or any one of the other similar labels. Partly as a quality control for this, and partly to facilitate comparison between programs and evaluation, the collection of at least a minimal amount of comparable data across programs is recommended. Until this is done, it becomes difficult to answer the basic and important question—who are the children being served—as well as the question of how these children are being served.

Dissemination and Overcoming Resistance

Given that there is much research yet to be done before the effectiveness of TFC programs can adequately be determined, how should the issues of dissemination and replication be pursued? These issues, along with the question of training, receive considerable attention in the present volume.

In considering this, it should be noted, as indicated earlier, that the research bases for the use of residential group treatment and the use of hospital treatment are at best still questionable. Yet these programs continue to operate, and in fact to grow (particularly in the private, for-profit sector). The evidence for the value of TFC, despite the shortcomings of the available data, is clearly sufficient to justify their continuation and even their growth.

It is to the credit of many developers of TFC programs that they express concern about the evaluation of their programs and that a few have even conducted such evaluations, but it is extremely important that more and better evaluation efforts be carried out. While these are going on, however, the appropriate attitude toward dissemination and replication should be a conservative one in which the potential new consumer is provided with the best available information on the effectiveness of both TFC and other alternative services. Then the potential consumer is in a position to make an informed judgment.

One of the peculiarities of the human services is that a kind of double standard is often applied to the evaluation of service programs. The standard applied in evaluating new programs is often much more demanding than the standard appplied for programs that have been in existence for longer periods of time.

This double standard partly reflects general resistance to change.

Proponents of TFC need to be sensitive to this. The services that are being offered differ in major ways from the more traditional residential and hospital programs with which most professionals are familiar. If the TFC efforts are to have a major impact on the field, then not only is better evaluative research needed, but responses of professionals will also need to change. This will take time and will require steady efforts to broaden the network of people familiar with the approach.

The combination of good data and efforts to involve and educate others in the field about TFC is likely to create a professional environment that is receptive to this innovation, and that provides an opportunity for it to have its maximum impact. This is particularly important because there is always a risk involved for policy makers when they provide resources to support new approaches rather than older, well-accepted approaches.

There is a particular risk involved with TFC, since the model calls for the placement of youngsters with serious emotional problems in open, family settings within the community. The conservative, safe approach is to continue to rely on more secure facilities, and on services that are better understood by professionals who have been long involved in the field.

From a system-of-care perspective, there is no need for the promotion of innovations to entail rejection of existing services. There are many youngsters with varied needs, and there is a role for a broad range of services within a continuum of care. Proponents of TFC can best advance their services by emphasizing their role within the system of care as the residential alternative that is typically most family oriented, least restrictive, least expensive, most normalized, and well worth trying for most youngsters before other residential services are used.

Summary

Overall, the growth of TFC programs represents an important and positive development in children's services. This thrust, still in its early stages, can make a major contribution toward improving services for youngsters, and toward challenging some of our assumptions about the kinds of services that youngsters need.

For this contribution to be fully realized, however, several issues need to be appropriately attended to:

1. An increased emphasis on the role of TFC within community-based systems of care. This will require that staff members of TFC programs become knowledgeable about the principles, components, and mechanisms of these systems. It will also require that staff members understand and appreciate the need for a range of services while recognizing the special and important contribution that TFC can make within such systems.

2. More and better efforts to evaluate the effectiveness of their programs. These efforts will have to include good descriptions of the children served in the program, the outcomes achieved (along several dimensions and over an extended period of time), and the costs. It will also require documentation that the program is not only serving a group of youngsters effectively but that it has an important role in a system of care; that is, that it is succeeding with youngsters who could not be just as adequately served in less expensive and less restrictive services. Evaluations should focus on TFC not just as an alternative to residential treatment but also in relation to regular foster care and intensive nonresidential services.

3. The task of creating an overall environment that is receptive rather than resistant to TFC services needs to be emphasized. Part of this process involves conducting evaluative research and participating in efforts by communities to build overall systems of care. The task also involves reaching out to policy makers and other professionals to inform them about the advantages of TFC services, the limitations, and the state of knowledge about them.

The TFC field has the promise of filling an important need in the children's services field. The early years of the field have produced many successes, but there are important challenges that must be met if the movement is to serve children, families, and the entire field well.

REFERENCES

Auclaire, P., and Schwartz, I. M. 1987. Are home-based services effective: A public child welfare agency's experiment. *Children Today* 16: 6–9.

Behar, L. 1986. A model for child mental health services: The North Carolina experience. *Children Today* 15: 16–21.

Curry, J. 1986. Outcome studies of psychiatric hospitalization and residential treatment of youth: Conceptual and research implications. Paper presented at annual meeting of the American Psychological Association, Washington, DC.

Edna McConnell Clark Foundation. 1985. *Keeping families together: The case for family preservation*. New York: Edna McConnell Clark Foundation.

Friedman, R. M. 1983. Therapeutic foster home programs in Florida: A mid-1982 status report. Unpublished manuscript, Florida Mental Health Institute, Tampa, FL.

———, and Street, S. 1985a. Admission and discharge criteria for children's mental health services: A review of the issues and options. *Journal of Clinical Child Psychology* 14: 229–235.

———, and ———. 1985b. Family-focused interventions: An annotated bibliography. Unpublished manuscript, Florida Mental Health Institute, Tampa, FL.

Gedeon, S. 1986. The parent-therapist program. Presentation made to meeting of project directors, Child and Adolescent Service System Program, Washington, DC.

Gutstein, S. 1987. Challenging myths about adolescent psychiatric hospitalization. Paper presented at annual meeting of the American Psychological Association, New York City.

Hawkins, R. P.; Fremouw, W. J.; and Reitz, A. L. A model useful in designing or describing evaluations of planned interventions in mental health. In *Practical program evaluation methods in youth treatment*, edited by A. J. McSweeny, W. J. Fremouw, and R. P. Hawkins. Springfield, IL: Charles C. Thomas, 1982.

———; Meadowcroft, P.; Trout, B. A.; and Luster, W. C. 1985. Foster family-based treatment. *Journal of Clinical Child Psychology* 14: 220–228.

Joint Commission on Mental Health of Children. 1969. *Crisis in child mental health*. New York: Harper and Row.

Kinney, J. W.; Madsen, B.; Fleming, T.; and Haapala, D. A. 1977. Homebuilders: Keeping families together. *Journal of Consulting and Clinical Psychology* 39: 905–911.

Kirigin, K. A.; Braukmann, C. J.; Atwater, J. D.; and Wolf, M. M. 1982. An evaluation of the Teaching-Family (Achievement Place) group homes for juvenile offenders. *Journal of Applied Behavior Analysis* 15: 1–16.

Knitzer, J. 1982. *Unclaimed children*. Washington, DC: Children's Defense Fund.

Lowman, R. L. 1987. Economic incentives in the delivery of alternative mental health services. Paper presented at annual meeting of the American Psychological Association, New York City.

Meadowcroft, P. M.,and Almeida, M. C., chairs. 1987. *Foster parents as treatment agents*. Symposium presented at the annual meeting of the American Psychological Association, New York.

O'Dell, S. 1974. Training parents in behavior modification: A review. *Psychological Bulletin* 81: 418–433.

Patterson, G. R. 1974. Interventions for boys with conduct problems: Multiple settings, treatments, and criteria. *Journal of Consulting and Clinical Psychology* 42: 471–481.

Phillips, E. L. 1968. Achievement Place: Token reinforcement procedures in a homestyle rehabilitation setting for "predelinquent" boys. *Journal of Applied Behavior Analysis* 1: 213–223.

Stroul, B. A., and Friedman, R. M. 1986. *A system of care for severely emotionally disturbed children and youth*. Washington, DC: Georgetown University Child Development Center.

United States Office of Technology Assessment. 1986. *Children's mental health: Problems and services—A background paper*. Washington, DC: U.S. Office of Technology Assessment.

Update. 1986a. Day treatment. *Update* 1 (2): 8–10.

Update. 1986b. Therapeutic foster care. *Update* 2 (1): 8–10.

Update. 1987. Case management. *Update* 2 (2): 10–12.

Webb, D. B. 1988. Specialized foster care as an alternative therapeutic out-of-home placement model. *Journal of Clinical Child Psychology* 17: 34–43.

About the Editors

ROBERT P. HAWKINS, PH.D, is a Professor and Coordinator of Child Clinical Training, Psychology Department, West Virginia University and is a consultant to the PRYDE program, which he and William Clark Luster began at the Pressley Ridge Schools. His particular interest has been in maximally relevant, minimally artificial, and thus community-based (in family and school) treatment for disturbed, disturbing, and retarded children and youth.

While teaching at the University of Washington, he and colleagues conducted the first experimental study of child treatment by in-home behavioral training of the parent. As a Research Fellow in the Bureau of Child Research at the University of Kansas he conducted direct intervention in both home and school settings for underprivileged and troubled youngsters. At Western Michigan University, he developed a school-based intervention program for severely disturbed/disturbing children and youth in Kalamazoo Valley Intermediate School District.

JAMES BREILING, PH.D., is a psychologist in the Antisocial and Violent Behavior Branch of the National Institute of Mental Health. He has primary responsibility for research and related activities on antisocial, violent, and sexual offending behaviors of children, youth, and adults. A special focus is the early identification of youth at high risk for progression to more serious antisocial behaviors. There is also special emphasis on the development, evaluation, and refinement of more effective, humane, and cost-effective models of treatment and management.

For more than a decade, Dr. Breiling has participated in the development of therapeutic foster care by encouraging research, convening meetings, and serving as the first chairperson of the advisory committee for the Foster Family-Based Treatment Association.